THE
BLESSED
LIFE

Luis R. Lugo, M.Th.

Published by:
L&L Publication
1301 Poplar Court
Homewood, IL 60430

DEDICATION

This book is dedicated to my son Kyle whose life has been one of illness and physical setbacks. Yet when I look at his life I see a blessed life in that he has encouraged most of our family to live life to its fullest. His zest for life, his willingness to search out opportunities for advancement and employment leaves some ashamed. Kyle always had something to offer even when he was ill. We knew when he was overcoming his illness because there would be a song coming from his lips.

His life always motivated and encouraged all those who were his nurses and took care of him. He has been an encouragement to members of the church as well as those who are his contemporaries. His humor and understanding of the technical aspects of life made understanding and using the computer and other electronic gadgets easy to understand. Even to the point of selling cars, photography and developing a recording studio, he has been an inspiration to my life and he has been my hero!

SPECIAL THANKS

Special thanks to Faydel Grayson for her typing of the notes, to Angela Wright for editing and typing the first manuscript.

To Brenda Gilbert for the final typing and correction.

Special thanks to Michael Owoke for the reading of the manuscript and for his encouragement.

TABLE OF
CONTENTS

FOREWORD

by Michael Awaoke

T*he Blessed Life* is a priceless jewel among the vast riches of God's grace. Dr. Lugo has done a superb job of taking each beatitude as a precious gem and polishing it for the reader to examine and put on for themselves; thereby, becoming a reflection of God's magnificent glory for all to see and behold.

In *The Blessed Life*, encouragement is given by the author to have us look at our lives and see what a true blessing is. He encourages us to look at how we can turn our trials into triumphs and how to take defeat and make them sweet victories.

The Blessed Life should be read by all and apply by all. It should be a book that is read over and over again until one begins to understand the vast principles of the Christian commitment as bestowed by Jesus in these beatitudes.

The Blessed Life is about the disciple's attitude and ministry of life. It teaches him how to so live and love that God will receive the Glory and the disciple will find pleasure in serving the God of this universe.

I therefore recommend this book to every member of the redemptive society of God and pray that it will enhance their lives and activities for God.

INTRODUCTION

T he Beatitudes suggest only what men for ages wished or dreamed of: A position in life where life would be a Utopia—where the pains, tragedies and misfortunes of life had no direct bearing on the type of life that one could live! It is precisely this state that the master Jesus addresses in this section of the Sermon on the Mount. Jesus is describing the basis and the conditions of that inner state of tranquility that mankind must have in order to survive in this world.

The tragedy of life can be seen in the pursuits that mankind makes. Ever since the dawn of creation he has sought through every means available that which will give his life meaning and purpose. His pursuit of that illusion called "happiness" is seen from day to day. Although this pursuit is noble in purpose *and thought*, it will ultimately lead him to ruin and shame. Man has sought happiness in things, wealth, and pleasure. He has searched the entire world for all its riches but is no better off. He has given himself to the pursuit of carnal fulfillment, political power, military power and intellectual sophistry and is no happier. He has tried alcohol, drugs, and crime, and he is still miserable. He has found more ways to kill himself trying to be happy than ever experiencing any form of true happiness! His pursuit will take many twists, turns and routes only to find that he cannot find that allusiveness called happiness. Happiness cannot be bought at the corner store. It cannot be gotten through any of the above means. As a matter of fact, true happiness is not really attainable, for God has something much better and greater in store for us than happiness. Jesus calls it **"Blessedness"**.

The word "Blessed" has a long and rich history. It is a word that conveys a state of being, rather than a mere fleeting momentary diversion from the realities of life! This term "Blessed" comes to us from the word "Makarios" used in the plural form in the Beatitudes. The word occurs in classical Greek as "Makar," an adjective describing the gods as opposed to mortals. Later it came to be used also of men, and especially of the blessed dead, who were liberated from the influence of the outside world.

Behind the original usage of the Greek word lay the idea that the gods were blessed in themselves, unaffected by the outside world. This condition of being blessed is ascribed to the gods by such writers such as Homer and Hesud, who spoke of the gods as distinct from men, who are liable to poverty and death. Thus, one general conclusion of the word "Makarios" originally meant that state which is neither produced nor affected by external circumstances, but is intrinsic within.

William Barclay says the meaning of the word "Makarios" can best be seen from one particular usage. The Greeks called the island of Cyprus "ho Makarios" which meant the "happy isle", and they did so because they believed that Cyprus was so lovely, so rich and so fertile an island that a man would never need to go beyond its coastlines to find the perfect, happy life. It had such a climate, such flowers and fruit and trees, such minerals and natural resources that it contained within itself all the materials for perfect happiness.

Makarios, then, described the joy which has its secret within itself, that joy which is serene and untouchable and self-contained, that joy which is completely independent of all the chances and changes of life!

This term "Blessedness" is descriptive of the state that Jesus expected for his disciples—a state where nothing that occurred out in the world would affect their perspective of the world. It described that sense of serene and utmost confidence. It made life a thing of unchanging realities. It denoted the level of Utopia that man is seeking, the state of finding oneself fortunate, well off, thriving and prosperous . . . that good condition which has nothing to do with the external conditions of life.

This word describes the fact that the Christians cannot seek happiness because happiness depends on the external circumstances, chances and changes of life. However, the Blessed Christian is totally untouchable and unassailable. It is a state of being that cannot be changed by accidents, but rather stands the test of pain, suffering and grief. It represents that state of relationship, which is a by-product of our relationship in Christ! This true, totally Blessed life cannot be found separate and apart from Christ! It is only when man sees the true nature of the type of attitude that God wants us to have, that we will find true happiness.

Previously the Beatitudes were seen as a vehicle for setting the virtues ordained by God for men. But now it is quite clear that phrases such as "poor in spirit", "those who mourn", "are meek", "hunger and thirst after righteousness" are merely different aspects of the type of attitude Christ requires of His disciples. It is not the virtuous which are important as much as the promise of salvation conveyed by the (blessed) at the beginning, as well as by the motive clause in the second half of each line.

Thus the blessed life is composed of the attitude, which the word introduces. Only those whose attitudes are reflected by the following clauses after the word "Blessed" are blessed.

What a state! It is a state that no one can rob or break through or steal because it is the by-product of a right relationship with the God who created the heavens and the earth.

What then should be man's s greatest drive in life? To secure such a relationship with God that it will produce "the Blessed life" —that life which is not dependent on the outward, external conditions of life, but which is equipped to rejoice in whatever circumstances it finds itself in.

What then is the cause for not having the "Blessed life"? Behind the lack of the Blessed life lies sin as the fountainhead of all misery and of holiness as the final and effectual curse for every woe. It is sin that robs us of our joy and true happiness in this life, and only by adequately dealing with sin can we find the full-blessed life. It is therefore imperative to recognize that without one dealing adequately with sin the blessed life is impossible. It is precisely this denial of sin which man seeks for that Utopia that will free him to enjoy the pursuits of happiness, while they are the very things that rob him ultimately of his joy!

Therefore man must adequately deal with his sin. It is only when he deals with his sin problem that he can enjoy the Blessed life. Therefore he must come to Christ on the terms of the Master. He must come through the prescribed will of God, which will eradicate sin in his life, and put him into a relational state that will provide for his continuous cleansing from sin because of a changed attitude.

How does man come to terms with God? First of all he must have faith. However, faith is a result of the *"hearing of the words of Christ"*. (Rom 10:17) Therefore, the first thing that man must do in order to acquire faith is the hearing of an unpolluted and unadulterated *Gospel*. This hearing is not just the act of listening but must be inclusive of understanding what he hears! This understanding should then elicit "conviction" or "trust" in God's Son as He who has been sent by God. Without this belief, man will ultimately perish (John 8:24). This belief must be more than intellectual assent. It must so motivate the individual that it will lead one to a "changing of the mind". This changing of the mind is effected by the knowledge that one receives as he or she understands that out of Christ, their relationship with God is non-existent. As one changes his mind, one is led to repentance. The effect of repentance comes when the mind is convicted of its sin, and the "will of the mind" is effectively changed. This change of will should produce a change in one's emotions—to the degree that it will produce a change in one's life! Without this complete change Jesus says, *"one will perish"* (Luke. 13:3-5). Once the change takes place, man must, in response to what he has heard, believed and changed his mind about (sin), reunite himself with God through the blood of Christ by being "baptized" for the forgiveness of his sins. (Acts 2:38) This baptism puts him into a right relationship with the Father, for in baptism, man declares his humility, his sin, his contrition of sin and his death to sin. It is here that the process of the blessed life begins. Man receives the *"seal of God"* (II Tim. 2:19) (Eph. 1:13-14) which is *'the gift of the Holy Spirit"* (Acts 2:38. Man is immediately "added to the church" (Acts 2:47; I Cor. 12:13). He can now begin to enjoy the privileges given only to those who are in the blessed life, "prayer, worship, fellowship and the Lord's Supper" (Acts 2:42). This rebirth is the start of the blessed life and to show that that is so, all one has to do is look at the very first attitude on which Jesus pronounces His *blessedness.*

MATTHEW 5:3

*Blessed are the poor in spirit; for
theirs is the kingdom of heaven.*

In this beatitude, the teaching of Jesus goes contrary to that in the expectant norm of human kind. Jesus, in this verse, goes to the taproot of man's problem—his egotistical pride. He reaches into that one element that man considers to be his greatest asset, his pride. Yet, Jesus smacks at the cornerstone of society's scorn that a humble man is a weak man, that he is a floor mat for everyone. Jesus sees "poorness in spirit" as the true gateway to the Blessed life. He views poorness in spirit as the blessed state of humility. Without this particular mind or mentality the Blessed life is an improbability and at best an exercise in futility!

Is there any real blessedness in being *poor*? Certainly there is nothing humble about abject poverty that leads to one's inability to provide for the necessities of life or for one's family.

There is nothing Blessed in being on welfare and the recipient of charity and the benevolent charity of individuals, unless being poor leads one to look for the God of heaven and to depend on him for sustenance!

William Barclay in his "Daily Study Bible Series" calls Matthew 5:3 "the supreme beatitude". Arthur Pink calls it "foundational". The reason for these two quotes is to illustrate the place that Jesus sought to give the proper disposition of character to the qualities that leads to the Blessed life. In order to fully comprehend "poor in spirit" one must have an understanding of what the term does not mean, as well as what it means.

Did Jesus mean to imply that sociological poverty is a condition of spirituality? Can there really be any true blessedness in being poor? There is no merit or advantage in being poor. Poverty does not guarantee spirituality; as a matter of fact material poverty can be a symptom for a disease called laziness, covetousness and resentfulness. Often times those who are poor in material things may be so because they are trusting in riches rather than God. Arthur Pink says: *"There is no virtue (and often no disgrace) in financial poverty as such, nor does it of itself produce humility of heart for anyone who has any real acquaintance with both classes soon* discovers there is just as much pride in the indigent as there is in the opulent." (116)

What then does Jesus mean by the usage of this term? First

of all we need to look at three words that are found within the scriptures that will enable us to understand the term "poor."

"Poor" in the Hebrew is found in the word "ani" which is the equivalent of the word used by Jesus to describe a man who "was nothing and because of it, he was despised and mistreated." This person had no power or influence as used in Luke 18 about the widow. He is one who has no friends and who therefore trusts wholly in God.

The Greek words that are used to designate the poor come to us from the words "Pener" and "Ptochos". Pener comes from the verb (Ponomai), which is related to Ponos, (pain) and Poneomai (to suffer pain). This word describes that man who is poor but he earns his daily bread by his own labor. Even though his labor brings pain, that is tiredness, he nevertheless can satisfy his poverty with his hands. This word describes the workingman who has nothing superfluous. He is not rich but he is not totally destitute. He must struggle daily to earn enough wages to satisfy his daily need. This man is called according to Barclay and Zodhiates (autodiakonos), a deacon to himself, one who ministers to himself. This word in reality does not indicate extreme want, that which verges upon it. It is the opposite of the rich who need not work to satisfy his needs.

On the other hand, the word Ptochos is one who no matter how hard he works cannot satisfy his needs. He is like Lazarus (Luke. 16-20-21), destitute. He is impoverished with no inherent ability to supply his needs. He is a welfare recipient in our time. He is one who is so destitute that he must have help from others or he dies. This word Ptochos is also related to the verb Ptoossein which means, "to crouch", as is the person who in his objectless ness needs to crouch in the presence of his superiors. Why then did Jesus select this term? The choosing of this term helps to convey to man the idea of this proper evaluation and condition of his and our place before a mighty savior. He is empty, destitute, and utterly helpless. His condition is of such a nature that all self-help is impossible and he must depend on those who have the power and the resources to come to his aid and help. Since Jesus is striving to bring man back into a proper relationship with God, his only true source of help can come from God.

Let us notice where the realm of this poverty is to take place. This poverty is a poverty of "spirit". Therefore, Jesus is not pronouncing a blessing upon an economic situation where people have little food to eat, no clothes to wear, and no shelter from which to escape the scourging of the elements. But rather he is describing the results which come when man comes into contact with God and sees himself as he truly is! He is totally destitute of any power; he has no self-assurance that he can in and of himself save himself from Hell. Jesus is concerned with man's attitude—his disposition towards his true condition before the God of the *Universe!* In this confrontation man's

disposition and attitude should be according to M. L. Jones –
"... *a complete absence of pride, a complete absence of self-assurance and self-reliance. It means a consciousness that we are nothing in the presence of God. It is nothing that we can produce; it is nothing that we can do ourselves. It is just this tremendous awareness of our utter nothingness as we come face to face with God.*"

Arthur Pink says: "*Poverty of spirit may be termed the negative side of faith. It is the realization of my utter worthlessness, which precedes the laying hold of Christ, the eating of His flesh and the drinking of His blood. It is the spirit emptying the heart of self, that Christ may fill it. It is a sense of need and destitution.*"

Zpiros Zodhiates says: "*What this Beatitude actually says is that unless man realizes his poverty, his complete emptiness and inability to fill the void, he will not be filled. If you don't realize you are sick, you will not seek a doctor nor will you take the medicine he might prescribe. Emptiness is necessary before fullness can take place. Only as we empty ourselves can God fill us with himself because of Christ and on account of Him. Thus we become whole. We become blessed. With the emptying of self and the filling of Christ, blessedness ensues, the blessedness of heaven in the human heart, even while on earth. For though this earth may produce distressing circumstances, they will not affect the conditions of the soul in any way. Thus we have the diagnosis, the medication and the results*" (p.66)

The place of this Beatitude shows us how important it is for one to recognize his true state before God. Man's true state is absolute destitution, the realization that we have nothing, we are nothing and without God, we will continue to be nothing. This should humble and give us the attitude of putting our whole trust in God. If we can come to this point in our thinking and activity it would help us to draw close to God and to move further away from the things which would separate us from having a proper relationship with God.

Without this attitude man cannot enter into the kingdom of heaven. This Beatitude therefore is placed first in order that we may fully understand that humility is the fundamental character of anyone who would stand and truly serve God. Without this aspect of humility, the rest of the Beatitudes would mean nothing, for they are the results of being destitute of spirit. There is a call for a thorough emptying of the cup before there can be a filling. We must understand that "poor in spirit" does not mean "poor spirited" and void of any real backbone. This Beatitude does not show any cowardliness and weakness on the part of him who so possesses it. On the contrary, this beatitude is reflective of an inner strength that comes from the recognition of our weaknesses. Humility is not weakness. Being poor in spirit is the opposite of the attitude of self-pride and self-assertion.

The classic example of humility is Jesus Christ and dare say that there has never been one who was as strong as he is. Who has ever reproduced those innate qualities that are found in Christ Jesus? Where is the person whose character of "toughness", "righteousness" and "fairness" have interwoven to create those tears and attitude, "not my will but thine be done!" Christ's example of humility is brought forth by Paul's prolific illustration as recorded in Phil. 2:5-8. "Have this mind in you which was also in Christ Jesus who existing in the form of God counted it not that being on an equal basis with God a thing to be grasped but he emptied himself. Taking the form of a servant being made in the likeness of man and being formed in fashion as a man, he humbled himself, becoming obedient even unto death, yea even the death of the cross." If there ever was a triumphant life it was the life of Jesus as He humbled himself into the very thing which he had created to the point that He allowed His own creation to take his life. It is this attitude of total surrender to the cause of God that Jesus addresses here.

The blessedness of poverty of spirit is further blessed with the unfailing promises of God. Jesus says that theirs is the "kingdom of heaven". If humility is the key to unlock the doors of the kingdom then pride is the lock that keeps one out. What does the Kingdom of Heaven mean? The word kingdom designates the rule, the reign, and the dominion of God. When a person humbles himself and enters into a proper relationship with God, He, God, then rules in the life of that individual. As God rules we are partakers of all the *Blessings of Heaven*. Only those who actually see their deep sense of futility will seek the kingdom of God. Only the humble will submit to the authority and supremacy of Jesus *Christ!*

MATTHEW 5:4

*Blessed are they that mourn for
they shall be comforted.*

T he natural succession of this verse is in perfect relationship in terms of the power of the gospel. The gospel must first convict before it corrects and brings comfort. The natural process when one is convicted of his own unworthiness before God would be to shed tears for our undone condition before God. It was the "poverty of spirit" that led Isaiah the prophet, of God's messianic message to cry out"... *Woe is me! For I am undone because I am a man of unclean lips and I dwell in the midst of a people of unclean lips . . .* "(Isaiah 6:5). What caused this spontaneous outburst of humility? Isaiah answers this question when he says "...for mine eyes have seen the King Jehovah of hosts." It was this confrontation with God and His Holiness vs. 3 that made Isaiah realize how destitute and bereft of any spiritual qualities He possessed before the God of Heaven. Isaiah's ability to recognize His unworthiness brought great comfort for him. In verses 6-7 one of the Seraphim flew unto Isaiah, "having a living coal in his hand, which he had taken with the tongs from off the altar; and he touched my mouth with it, and said, Lo, this has touched thy lips; and thine iniquity is taken away, and thy sin forgiven."

It was no wonder when God needed someone he could send, Isaiah volunteered, *"here am I, send me!"* (vs 8).

This incident in the life of the messianic prophet parallels the sinner's experience when true confrontation with the sinner takes place and genuine introspection of one's self takes place. Man must invariably realize how utterly bereft and destitute before God he is.

In the Beatitudes, this natural progression is like a well-fitted staircase that allows the other qualities to show forth.

Since Jesus has laid the foundation Beatitude as humility of spirit, the next logical step would be man's response to his sinful condition and how far from God he has departed. This should strike at the chords of one's heart and bring forth a river of sincere tears for one's true circumstance.

What did Jesus mean when he pronounced a blessing on those who mourn? In order for us to fully comprehend this Beatitude, we must understand the term that Jesus used when he pronounced this blessing upon mankind:

The Greek word for mourn (Penthountes)—portrays sorrow of the acutest type. Liddle and Scott say it means "to bewail, lament and mourn." Thayer says it means to "mourn, weep, and lament." This word literally means to weep audibly, to shed tears, to cry as a child. The word sobbing is a fitting description of this word and what it conveys.

This word is one of the strongest words for mourning in the Greek language. It is the word used for the mourning in the Greek language. It is the word used for the mourning of the dead, for the passionate lament for one who was lived. It is the kind of grief, which takes such a hold on a man that it cannot be hidden. It is that type of sorrow that pierces the heart and expresses itself in the audible crying and shedding of tears. It is intense sorrow. It is the sorrow that brings pain to the heart that leaves a person to grieve and literally takes possession of the whole person and it cannot be concealed. The great noted preacher Chrysotam described these words as the 'mourning ones" who are so grieved that their grief manifests itself openly." What is it that can so bring a man to such a state that as he humbles himself before God, his soul brings forth such mourning? I believe it is that thing for which we as a society, nation and a people have disdain—*sin!* The falling short of God's mark. Our inability to be perfect and without smear. Sin has lost its abhorrence in the sight of a society bent on refusing to acknowledge the supremacy of God, and as man looks for the joy of life, he finds that the very thing that offers him that joy, (sin) causes him untold misery. Sin is a problem that man must face. He cannot deny the reality, or its stronghold. He must see it for what it is! An evil that brings forth spiritual death and total separation from a holy God who has no desire to see the sinner lost. Sin as defined in the scriptures is a violation of God's law (I John 3:4). It is doing unrighteousness (I John 5:17). It is missing the mark (Ro 3:23). However one aspect of sin that we have often failed to see is what sin does to God. Sin is a tremendous problem to God. In the book of Genesis the 6th chapter, verse 6 *"and it repented God Jehovah that he had made man on the earth and it grieved him at his heart."* Why did God repent or what caused him to grieve? The answer is found in verse 5. *"And Jehovah saw that the wickedness of man was great in the earth, and that every imagination of the thoughts of his heart was only evil continually."* It was sin that broke and grieved the heart of God. When we come to the realization of what sin truly is, and what it does to our heavenly Father who cannot utterly fall down in deep mourning for our sins? How can one face a God of "mercy, love, compassion and a willingness to forgive mankind of his sins," and not be touched to the point that one falls to one's face in bitter remorse and mourning for one's shortcomings and transgressions? Sin is a serious thing and a serious problem for God.

How the World Views Mourning

Our world seems to despise anyone who has enough sensibility to shed tears and feel a sense of contrition. It decries and calls that spirit of genuine mourning and contrition as "weakness and foolishness". Not realizing the inherent potential for absolute peace and comfort that results from a genuine conversion. To the world, mourning is an act of human dependency on a power that is neither believed in nor acceptable, nor is trust in a book that is seen as mythological and full of fancy stories.

This lack of sensitivity shows the cruelty and coldness of the world. It shows that the world has gotten so removed from God that any type of action that makes it realize the Supremacy of God causes it discomfort. In the day of Ezekiel the Prophet, God showed Jerusalem the fact that she was "worse" than Sodom in this respect. Behold this was the iniquity of thy sister Sodom, Pride, fullness of bread hold this was the iniquity of thy sister Sodom, Pride, fullness of bread and prosperous ease was in her and in her daughter. Neither did she strengthen the hand of the poor and the needy! (Ezek. 16:4-9). Our society has grown fat and her wealth and pride will not allow her to mourn for the affliction of her self and her brother, Jacob, and anyone who will is a negative voice in the wilderness. The world does not want to deal with guilt for if they deal with guilt, they must acknowledge the reality of sin. To acknowledge the cross of Christ is to acknowledge the supremacy of God and the destitution of man. Therefore the world views those who mourn over their sins as weaklings rather than acknowledging God's supremacy.

Who are the blessed mourners? There are three types mentioned in the New Testament; they are the natural, the sinful and the gracious mourners.

When we deal with **natural sorrow** we are dealing with the sorrow that is brought about by the loss of a loved one, dashed hopes, or financial reverses. The Bible, in Rom. 12:15, tells us "to weep with those who weep." When a tragedy occurs, our hearts should be moved with compassion and our hearts should be melted together with those who have had a misfortune to happen to them. How can we hold back our bowels of mercies and not reach out in their affliction?

When we speak of **sinful mourning** we are speaking of that which the Bible calls "worldly sorrow" (II Cor. 9:7-10). This worldly sorrow is not based on a genuine fact finding repentance of wrong, but rather it is a sorrow brought about by the consequences one suffers for violating the dictates and laws of the world. This sorrow is not godly. Given the opportunity to try the same thing again, the offender would offend again.

The Bible teaches that Judas after his treachery was uncovered, went out and hanged himself. The reason that is given for this suicide is "repentance," but was it "godly sorrow"? No. His sorrow was in the fact that he had been discovered to be both a thief and a traitor. Peter, on the other hand, performed no less despicable act than Judas, but when faced with the heinousness of his denial, he did not just go out and weep bitter tears. Instead, he sought forgiveness from the master and he went on to become a mighty force for God. What was the difference in both of these men's actions? The motive. One could not stand the fact he had offended God, while the other was upset that he had gotten caught.

This worldly sorrow is portrayed day in and day out in our penal systems. Men who have stolen do not sorrow because they have stolen, but because they have gotten caught. One on death row who has deliberately and without any pangs of conscience taken the life of another, cries not for his actions, but for the mere fact that he has been caught and now faces the consequences of having his life taken in exchange for the one he has taken. Consider the homosexual or that adulterous man and woman, or junkie full of various diseases, are they mourning for their sins, or are they mourning because of the consequences of their sins?

This sorrow, worldly sorrow, brings forth death. It is a regret that will not change the mind nor affect a change in the lifestyle of the individual.

The third type of sorrow is a **sorrow** that is **produced because of godliness**. It is a sorrow that recognizes the ultimate good of God and one's deficiency before Him. It is that realization of emptiness that stares one in the face and breaks him into dust before God. It is a Paul striving to overcome that war in his eternal members who in sheer need of deliverance cries out, *"Wretched man that I am who shall deliver me!"* It is when one comes to the realization that they have broken and violated God's heart that causes them to turn away in shame and in tears and seek God's forgiveness. It is that sorrow that *"Draws nigh to God and He draws nigh to one."* It is that sorrow that will compel one to *"cleanse ones hands and purify one's mind."* It is that sorrow that will make one to *"be afflicted, mourn and weep and turns whatever joy one may have into mourning and to heaviness."* It is that sorrow that *"humbles one in the sight of God and brings about ones exaltation."*

This sorrow is not only for one's sins but it also compels one to see the sins of one's brethren and of the world and of the injustices that bring much sorrow on my part. Listen to the apostle Paul as he expresses these sentiments: *"I say the truth in Christ, I lie not, my conscience bearing within me in the Holy Spirit, that I have great sorrow and increasing pain in my heart, for I could wish that I myself was anathema from Christ for brethren's sake, my kinsmen according to the flesh, who are Israelites, whose is the adoption, and the glory and the covenants and the giving of the law and the service of God and the promises; whose are the fathers, and of whom is Christ as concerning the flesh who is over all, God blessed for ever. Amen."* (Rom. 9:1-5).

Why was Paul in sorrow for the Jew? In Romans Chapter 10:1—4, he gives us the reason why he mourned for the sins of his people.

"Brethren my heart's desire and supplication to God is of them that they might be saved. I bear this witness that they have a zeal of God, but not according to knowledge. For being ignorant of God's righteousness and seeking to establish their own they did not subject themselves to the righteousness of god. For Christ is the end of the law unto righteousness to everyone that believeth."

Paul's sorrow was for the sins of pride and prejudice that Israel manifested. In so doing they rejected the Messiah and would lose their salvation through Christ. Paul sorrows for this to the point that he wished he could have become a substitute upon the altar of sacrifice if it would bring about the salvation of his nation. This type of sorrow produces men like David when faced by Nathan the Prophet. It causes a Jeremiah to weep over Jerusalem. It causes an apostle to go into the night to weep bitterly. It causes a Jesus of Nazareth to cry out over a city and to climb the hill of Golgotha after undergoing the insults of a mocked trial, a frightful beating and the ridicule of those whom he had made and to stretch forth his hands to be pierced by trained experts in the field of crucifixion and, with one blow, nail innocent hands and feet to the cruelty of the cross, to endure its shame, receive the insults of tail waggers and condemned criminals and still with enough love and compassion, forgive a thief and ask forgiveness for those whom he had cried over.

But Jesus does not stop by pronouncing a blessed mourner; He tells us why the mourners are blessed. "They shall be comforted." How is one comforted? Because one does what is needed to get rid of the sin that divides one from God. A mother suffers much pain during childbirth, but joy cometh after delivery. And so it is with sin. When it is repented of and confessed, there comes a peace of knowing that one is clean, has been washed in the Blood of the Lamb, and is free from the burden of sin.

The Blessed mourner is one who is comforted by God. As some have said, "Woe to him whose heart is so selfish that is incapable of feeling guilt, the tearless eye and the thoughtless heart are themselves causes for deep mourning."

MATTHEW 5:5

*Blessed are the meek for they shall
inherit the earth.*

The natural progression of Jesus in this ladder of the Blessed life brings us to one of the most paradoxical of all teachings. To many, the meek person is one who is in all areas really a weak person, one who never gets angry and if he does, he stifles it. The world views the meek person as flabby, milk toast, spineless and cowardly, very indecisive and afraid to get involved with the tidal waves of problems. He is viewed as one who is afraid to tackle those who are aggressive and vindictive towards him. This view of meekness comes because the worldview is one of being aggressive, egotistical, and self-serving. It is the attitude of indifference to one's feelings and concerns. However, this distorted view has not brought about any real change to our world.

In the natural progression of the Lord's beatitudes we

notice that the first thing one must do is to realize our own inability, which causes us to humble ourselves; we must realize just how exceedingly sinful sin is and causes us to mourn for our sins. These two conditions are essential if we are to get into a proper and right relationship with God.

While meekness is not a step necessary to salvation, it is, however, the results of God working in our life as a step towards Christ likeness; basically what we call the sanctification process for meekness is a "fruit of the spirit" (Gal. 5:23).

The word meekness is difficult to define by any one word. The word "meek" comes from the Greek work "Praus" which is related to the Hebrew (Anaw) and means humble, holy, meek, gentle (humility of the heart). It is this definition that has caused the misunderstanding of this rich word. The word as found in the classical usage was used of the capturing of a wild horse or eagle whose power and strength was brought under control. This power was never lost or killed. But rather the power was redirected to where it would serve the greater purpose. This word has some scientific analysis. The scientist takes a wild raging river, channels it into a dam, slows down its fury and lights up a city. All the raging power is still there. Remove the dam and that water which produces light for a city becomes death to the city in its wild, savage fury. So it is with the natural power of man. Unchecked it is destructive and deadly, but put to use in the proper way under the proper controls; it is a reservoir of unlimited power. Thus, the word meekness could and should be described as power or strength under control. It is that power of man brought under God's control and in conformity with God's word.

To illustrate that this is so, notice some of God's great Biblical characters that possessed this meekness, yet who would dare say that they were flabby, weak kneed, spineless wonders?

Moses was called the meekest man on earth (Num. 12:3) yet which of those Jews would stand in the way of this great leader once his anger was forced? Ask Pharaoh if Moses was weak. Ask any Egyptian if Moses was weak. No, Moses had submitted his will to God. He had put all of his power and ability under the dominion and ruler ship of God and was immortalized.

Recall Peter, who in the moment when the master was being taken prisoner, arises with sword in hand to cut off the ear of the servant. And of course there is Jesus who is our classic example of meekness (Matt. 11-28-30). Yet, it was this same Jesus who entered Jerusalem like a king, cleansed the temple and took no prisoners. It was He who in the synagogue heals a man and looks at those religious bigots with anger at the "hardness of their heart". Jesus displayed meekness. Meekness is anger at the right thing at the right time. It is not the cowardly retreating of confrontation and escaping the heat of battle. It is knowing when and where to get angry. It is that ability to have that God given strength under control.

Meekness possesses certain qualities, which are essential for the proper type of meekness to come *forth*. Meekness has two objects: (1) God and (2) Man. In meekness toward God there are those qualities of humility and sorrow for sin. It is the acknowledgment of the superiority of God and man's recognition that he is totally inadequate in and of himself to overcome sin and to give his life any sense of true direction. It is in this realm where true meekness takes place. This meekness allows God to rule supremely in one's life irrespective of the circumstances that may prevail. It is the attitude of Job: *"The Lord giveth, the Lord taketh, blessed be the name of the Lord"* (Job 1:21). It is that attitude that allows an apostle Paul to speak of thorns in the flesh and then burst out in a doxology of the Grace of God (II Cor. 2:1-10). It is this disposition as exemplified in the life of Christ, as he wrestles with the agony of the cross, "not my will but Thine be done" (Luke. 22:42). It is that attitude of mind that even though one may not fully understand the ultimate outcome, one nevertheless puts supreme and utmost confidence in the power of God.

It is that disposition that surrenders totally to the will of God and allows nothing to hinder, alter or affect one's relationship to God (Rom. 8:35ff). It is the disposition of slave and master, where we as the slaves are totally dependent on

God for our lives. Therefore meekness is not weakness, but it is the survival of the fittest, those who are suited for the work and ways of *God*!

But meekness must also be directed towards men and it is here where abuses concerning our understanding sometimes abound. In expressing meekness towards our fellow man we should "be gentile": In Gal. 6:1, *"Brethren if a man be overtaken in a fault, ye which are spiritual restore such a one in the spirit of meekness; considering thyself lest thou also be tempted"*. We are to be concerned and recognize that I we are our brother's keeper. I should be concerned enough that when one gets wounded in the battle, he can count on me to help him. My help, however, should be done in such a way that it would express itself in tender concern for one who has fallen. This disposition of restoration should be done not with haughtiness or vindictiveness but with total concern for the total restoration of my fallen brother. It should never be in the attitude of the Elder Brother, (Luke. 15) but it should be with the disposition of this one is ill let us treat him with the Balm of Gilead. Secondly, we should be obedient to authority as it has been ordained of God. The scriptures abound with the need and with the teaching that God expects Christians to be obedient to the civil laws of the land. These laws have been ordained of God and have so that we may live in a society where there is fairness. Notice Rom. 13:1, *"Let every soul be subject unto the higher powers for there is no power but of God; the power that be ordained of God." Tit. 3:1 "Put that in mind to be subject to principalities and powers, to obey magistrates to be ready to every good work." 1 Pet.2:13-14, "Submit yourselves to every ordinance of man for the Lord's sake whether it be to the King as Supreme or unto governor as unto them that are sent by him for the punishment of evildoers, and for the praise of them that do well."*

In our meekness towards men we are to be obedient to the laws of the land. This includes such things as stopping at red lights, stop signs, yield at yielding signs and doing the speed limit. These things may seem trite and they may be, but nevertheless we are to obey them. The meek person submits himself to these things not because he likes them or agrees with them, but he is under the control of God and he therefore renders obedience to the Law because of who he is rather that if he agrees with them or does not agree with them.

Now this is not a compulsory submission in the sense if it says 55 and on the speedometer I'm doing only 55, but in my head I'm doing 70. No it is the disposition that loves to do what is right. Jesus paid taxes to Caesar, Matt. 17:24-27, and his disposition was not one of anger or bitterness, but one of "let us not offend." Let's comply with the *Law*! So we too should have the same disposition.

No greater example of the meekness of a child of God can be evidenced than that of Paul; he lived in the world and had renounced it to his advantage as seen in Acts 22:24-30, and then in Acts 25:11. Paul used the Law lawfully because he had kept the Law as a private citizen, and knew how to as it does not conflict with the Laws of God. We must respect it, be obedient to it and support it to the best of our ability.

In our own meekness towards men we must control our anger towards them. The Bible gives us some insight into the controlling of our anger towards individuals. Proverbs 16:32, *"he that is slow to anger is better than the might; and he that ruleth his spirit than he that taketh a city."* Certainly we all get angry and the Bible does not forbid anger, for Paul said, be ye angry and sin not" (Eph. 4:26). But our anger should be under control. We must remember that "the wrath of man worketh not the righteousness of God" (James 1:20). We must not be so angry with our fellow man that it causes us to commit murder in our hearts against them (Matt. 5:21-22), but rather we should have the right type of anger against them. We first of all must have a cause. That is proper reason for our anger. Our anger should not arise because of bitterness or jealousy or envy, but rather as exemplified by Jesus in Matt. 21:12, when he saw the House of God being misused in its intended purpose. Our righteous indignation should always pour forth but never in the interest of revenge or retaliation. Meek Christians will always allow God to "avenge them" (Rom. 12:19), but his anger against his fellow man must be with constructiveness and should always be tempered with gentleness and forbearance. Remember that a horse does not lose his power because he has a bridle in his mouth, he is just under control.

Finally our meekness towards men must be evidenced in our attempts to teach them the ways of God. As God's people we must come to the conclusion that we have a religion that is predicated on us teaching it to others. As we teach, it should be done with sincere meekness. Peter in I Pet. 3:15 says, *"but sanctify the Lord God in your hearts; and be ready always to give an answer to every man that asketh you a reason of the hope that is in you with meekness and fear"*. Our answers to individuals who recognize that our behavior is based on "reasons" should never be given unreasonable answers or given one in an abrasive and cruel manner, but rather one that answered in a manner that is befitting the character and motive of a child of God.

Secondly, as we teach we should "not strive" (2 Tim. 2:24). That is to say, I should not have a spirit of contentiousness or fighting a factious spirit. It is not a physical fight but rather one that is based on reason and logic. As we teach, it should not be a quarrel, but one that is based on love and reason and provable assertions.

Meekness then affects every facet of our lives. As it pertains to God it should be a willingness to learn (Jas. 1:21) trusting

Him completely and being in submission and obedient to authority, controlling our anger, and having teaching characterized in control of total meekness.

The blessedness of the meek, they shall inherit the Earth. Much confusion has arisen as to the proper meaning of this phase, which is a quotation from Ps. 37:9. Those whose views are "millinestic" (pre or post) look forward to the day when Christians will have complete dominion over this earth. But we must not be misled by literal interpretations of spiritual attitudes when the Blessings are pronounced for possessing those qualities. This is not a future blessing but is something that is transpiring right here and now.

Let's look at the way God has used this form of blessing to inspire His people. God utilized the land as future inheritance for Abraham when he made the three-fold promise in Genesis 12 and in Genesis 13:14-17. It was this land promise which has led to so much fighting between the Arabs and Jews.

There are those who are still waiting for the fulfillment of this promise. But in Jos. 21:43 Joshua records that *"Jehovah gave unto Israel all the land which he swore to give their fathers..."* This land full of milk and honey would be given for a blessing and their enjoyment. This phrase then became synonymous with great blessings received from God. Everything that the father possesses is by right the children's inheritance. Therefore Paul says that all possessions are ours (I

Cor. 8:21-24). Now we may not possess anything "yet we possess all things" (2 Cor. 6:10). We have unclaimed possessions which we have failed to claim and therefore miss out on the great blessings of God. The Psalmist declared *"The meek shall eat and be satisfied"* (Ps. 21:26). The Lord lifts up the meek (Ps. 147:6). And "The meek shall increase their joy in the Lord (Ps. 21:26). These views show us that the meek enjoy their great blessings of God. Now the inheritance of the earth is not referring to this lasting forever, but it is the fulfillment of the "new heavens and the earth" (II Pet. 3:1-13). This old world will be burned up and in its place shall come the new heaven and the new earth. What is the new heaven and new earth? It was the cessation of the old Jewish kingdom and economy and the ushering in of the kingdom of Christ wherein we possesses all things. All the spiritual benefit of God belongs to the meek. Everything is ours. We are the victors— we claim it by right of son ship and meekness!

Matthew 5:6

Blessed are they who hunger and thirst after righteousness for they shall be filled.

I n the pronouncement of this Beatitude there could be no misunderstanding for if ever a people understood the significance of being hungry and thirsty, it was these who lived in this region of heat and desert. Yet Jesus is not appealing to the two most basic of man's needs in the physical element but rather as they are related with the rest of the Beatitudes. It seems as if the natural progression of the Beatitudes gets more demanding as our Lord points out the principles by which He will accomplish his task in saving the world.

In the first Beatitude Jesus points out that we must empty ourselves of any real or imagined power. In the second Beatitude he points out the need for realizing our true condition in sin. Then in the third Beatitude he points out the fact that we are now ready to listen since God has taken control of our lives. In the fourth Beatitude Jesus describes the attitude, which must be ours in our determination to attain the righteousness that God would have us to attain. This is one of the keys to living the Blessed life. That which is physically man's greatest need must become his greatest need in spiritual life.

The words that Jesus uses give us some insight into the challenge of being hungry and thirsty. The word "hungry" is from the Greek word "Peinao". This word means the hungering ones. It means to suffer, to be in want, to be needy, to seek, to have an eager desire. It is a famishing craving after, being destitute of having. Thirst comes from the word "dep sao," which means to suffer from want, to suffer thirst, to long for, to feel painfully.

Jesus is using the two most powerful tools that man possesses. A hungry and thirsty man who may possess the world's goods will eventually give all that he has to have his hunger fed and his thirst quenched. So must the child of God possess the disposition that he must so hunger after the righteousness of God, that he would give everything that he possesses in order to attain it. These two words then imply a strong craving and desire for the Righteousness of God.

We must really understand how hunger will cause a person to go beyond the legal methods to try and sustain his hunger. In this Gospel of John 6—the multitudes followed Jesus because He provided a sense of fulfillment of their hunger.

They followed him not because of the miracle he performed but because they ate the leaves which he had provided. Hunger was a way of life for the people that Jesus spoke to. If a man did not work he would not eat. This was a daily chore. This was a daily necessity. Some of the Master's greatest teachings had to do with hunger and thirst. As He traveled and the multitudes followed, He saw them as sheep without a shepherd, who could and would lead them to pastures green. He was compassionate because they hungered and He fed them because he feared they would faint if He sent them away, or as he spoke his parables they are either filled with food or water.—The Parable of the "Wheat and the Tares" and The Parable of the "Sower" (Matt. 13:16-30), the teaching of the Samaritan woman (John 4)—the feeding of the multitudes (John 6)—Lazarus (John 16)— the Lord's Supper (John 13). These and many teachings bring us into contact with the necessity of hunger and thirst. Even the great lessons or sacrifice dealt with the lack of eating and drinking (see Matt.4). So the Jews could relate quite well to being hungry and thirsty.

In our daily lives we exercise these two elements. In our society we are used to eating three to five meals a day. Yet the following day we will eat the same amount of meals. The same can be said for our drinking. We have plenty of water that is natural and in those areas where there may be a lack of natural drinking water; we have the technology to manufacture water.

So to a majority of us we have never identified with the sensation of not having a square meal or being deprived of drinking water; only when some great catastrophe like a hurricane, earthquake or tornado befalls us do we get a picture of being really hungry and thirsty.

Being hungry and thirsty serves as a barometer of health and strength for us. Usually one sign of illness is a lack of appetite. A lack of appetite says we are not feeling well. Something is wrong somewhere. Therefore, when we find a lack of appetite in our children we assume something is wrong and we seek help to find out what's wrong. The lack of appetite is also a sure sign that a sick person is not recovering from his illness. A strong, healthy appetite shows that life is present and that in order for the body to continue to function as it should, it must be fed well. In the same manner in

order for the soul to remain healthy it must constantly be fed and given to drink. If the spiritual pursuit of righteousness is not fed, it will soon die of malnutrition and cease to become a reality.

Hungering and thirsting after righteousness is sustained by a steady diet of God's word. The step into righteousness begins by faith. Faith is acquired through the assimilation of God's word (Rom. 10:17). In order for us to gain righteousness, we must never become self-satisfied with one meal. Righteousness does not happen overnight. Righteousness is a product of sanctification, which is a lifetime obsession. Our lives must reflect the divine nature of Christ and to this end we must feed our souls every day.

When we hunger and thirst after Righteousness and readily seek after it, we will get our priorities in line. Just like a cook cannot cook a meal without pots, pans and food, neither can we step into righteousness without having our priorities in proper perspective. We must *"lay aside every weight and sin that so easily besets us"* (Heb.12: 1), and put our eyes on Jesus. We must stop comparing ourselves to each other and compare ourselves to Christ! In so doing we shall see how far we fall short of His righteousness, that we will never be satisfied until we achieve that mark of the High Calling, which is the standard by which we must compare ourselves to Christ and strive for His righteousness. We must understand that there is no righteousness, separate and apart from the righteousness of Christ. His righteousness is an imputed righteousness. His righteousness is the sanctifying process as we are changed by the life of Christ into the divine image. This change cometh as a result of our faith in Christ (Phil. 3:6-11). It is separate and apart from any works of merit that we may be able to perform and is achieved by our trust and confidence in Christ Jesus (Gal. 3:26-27). This righteousness is all of the righteousness of God. The word "Diahaiasunem" means integrity, virtue, purity of life. It carries the intent of the proper thinking, feeling and character. It denotes not only doing what is right but being right also. This word is closely associated with the word justification. Our justification before God takes place in the sacrificial work of Christ by which salvation is offered to man. This salvation comes as a result of hearing, believing the gospel, repenting of our sins, confessing the son ship of Christ and being immersed for the forgiveness of sin. When we comply by faith, then God frees us from the bondage of sin and adds us to His body, the church. It is in this vein that God pronounces our righteousness as we endeavor to live the life of Christ! Righteousness is our walk in Christ. It is the manifestation of an inward cleansing and a burning desire to become more like Jesus. It is the death of the decaying man while the new man is created in the image of Christ. It is that Godlike character that respects and reverences the "things that are Godly" and treats fellows as if "they were better than self". It is the attitude of gratitude and of a working spirit that utilizes every opportunity to glorify God. This is hungering and thirsting. It is never complacent about moral achievement or satisfied with the knowledge of God's word. Everyday a study of God's word is essential. Everyday an opportunity to demonstrate God's work in our lives is sought for. What was learned yesterday and what works of God were done will not suffice for today.

Man must be careful, however, that he does not fall into

the trap of the Jews who instead of glorying in the righteousness of God, sought to establish and glorify in the own righteousness (Rom. 10:3). How did they do this? They did it with
an over extension of their own importance. Because of their
election as God's chosen, having the living oracles of God, they
felt that God owed them! Instead of humility and piety, they
exalted and gloried in their keeping not only of the law but in
the keeping of the laws of traditions as handed down by the
elders and scribes. It was this attitude, which allowed their
hearts to become hard and to exalt themselves and to put God
in a position of owing them for their ability to keep the Law.
Within this framework "they made void the word of God"
through their traditions and instead of teaching the word of
God, then embellished the thoughts and teachings of Rabbis
and refused to listen to the Truth. This crystallization of
human concepts led them to reject crystal clear interpretations
of prophecies, the subsequent denial of Jesus as the Messiah
and his ultimate crucifixion. If it had stopped here it would
have been sufficient, but this mentality carried over to the
rejection of the preaching of the gospel as well as the justification by grace of the death of Christ on Calvary's cross. This
same mentality caused untold damage to the infant church as
well as to the furtherance of the gospel.

May we add here that the self righteousness of man, separate and apart from the saving work of Jesus will always cause

a rejection of the Doctrine of Grace, and a sanctification and the work of the Holy Spirit in the life of the individual. It will always lead more to the basic denial of the need of salvation and in the end will cause his soul to be lost!

Self-righteousness then is the exaltation of the absolute goodness of man and the ability to keep adequately the letter of the law while rejecting the spirit of the law. This was the problem of the Jews who rejected the teaching of Christ as he applied the Law and gave it its proper meaning.

To the self righteous Jew, the fact they could be wrong was incomprehensible; that he would have to abandon his traditions and humble himself at the feet of the cursed cross was to him ludicrous. Nevertheless if one is to obtain the blessed life one must abandon his own self righteousness and accept the indispensable righteousness of God which is imputed and accept the fact that our justification is dependent upon the work of Christ and our hunger and thirst after righteousness must be our goal in life.

The master himself assures the blessed provision of being satisfied. That promise is that those who are actively seeking the righteousness of God "shall be filled..." This is the satisfaction of "hungering and thirsting after righteousness".

The word "filled "chortadzo" was originally applied to the gorging and fattening of animals in their lives. As it relates to man it carries the idea of the total and comprehensive satisfaction of that spiritual hunger and thirst. As used here it is a continuous process. Just as man provides for his daily food daily, and is satisfied, so it is with the hungering and thirsting. It is a continuous process. It is the sense of walking in the light and having continuous fellowship with *God.*

The question is how does God satisfy man's hunger and thirst after that which cannot be totally attained? The scriptures speak of the peace that passeth all understanding. The greatest gift that comes to those who are seeking God's righteousness is peace. This peace is not the absence of conflict but rather it is the confidence of knowing Jesus and as a result of a relationship with Him. This peace is supreme confidence *"that all things will work out for my benefit"* because of *"whom I have believed"* (II Tim. 1:12). It does not matter the difficulty of my situation, since God is in control and I once have yielded my life to Him, everything will work out fine. I have the promise that if I seek "God and His kingdom" first, Matthew 6:33 that I will have the necessities of life supplied. See also (Phil. 4:19). I have the assurance of God's perpetual forgiveness and fellowship (I John 1:7). I have the perfect provision of knowing that my prayers are heard (Rom. 8:26-28), that I have an advocate with the father, Jesus Christ the Righteous (I John 1:2). And I can be filled with the knowledge that I have had, I have now, and I will have life eternal (I John 5:12). What perfect provision from the perfect Father for the perfect *cause!*

MATTHEW 5:7

Blessed are the merciful for they shall obtain mercy.

The first four Beatitudes have so far been that which is geared to make a man look at himself from an internal perspective. He begins this introspective look by becoming keenly aware of his spiritual poverty. This spiritual poverty confronts him with the basic issue that *"all of his righteousness is but a filthy rag before God"*. He realizes how utterly destitute his life without the Divine Presence is. He therefore humbles himself and acknowledges the supremacy of God and his own poverty. This humbling of self then brings him into the reality of how sinful sin is and how he has hurt the creator and sustainer of the universe. This leads him to mourn for his sin as well as the sin of those who violate and are defiant in their attitude toward God. As we mourn for our sins we are confronted with the fact that our power is insufficient in and of itself, and that our power is of no value unless it is brought under the control of God. This control is called meekness. It is the surrendering to and our relying on the power of God. This poverty of spirit, mourning for our sins, our meekness makes us realize our need for a spiritual appetite, which makes us hunger and thirst after the righteousness of God. Since God has promised to satisfy our hunger, then, forgiveness of sins takes on a new dimension. We now look towards our fellow man. And in the following Beatitudes we find the fruits of the spirit as they are developed under the four headings of being "merciful, pure, peacemakers, and persecuted." We can then categorize these eight beatitudes in pairs of four. The first four are those basic needs of men and the second four deals with our disposition as a result of the first four.

This Beatitude has been misunderstood by some who seem to think that we "show mercy in order to receive mercy" when the reason for showing mercy is because we have experienced the mercy of God. This Beatitude as it follows the natural order must have been somewhat disconcerting to the multitudes. For the ancients in essence being merciful was a sign of weakness and an act that lacked backbone! The Great Roman despised pity and looked upon those who felt so as dangerous to the empire's global conquest. As one looks at the ancient world, one immediately is appalled at the total disregard for the unfortunate ones of life. The Roman Empire had some sixty million slaves and life was considered very cheaply. As a matter of fact, life was not considered among some. A child born deformed had no expectation of living. If the child was born a female, she stood as much chance of living as a cripple. To the Roman mindset, life was cheap and should be used to fulfill their wanton pleasure by inflicting cruelty. Total disregard for the taking of life is best seen in the theaters of Rome as "gladiators" fought to the death as the Roman population screamed and clamored for the shedding of blood on the defeated warrior.

As much as the Romans' thirst for blood was based on the absence of any real affection for its sacredness, the Pharisees of Jesus' day were cold-hearted legalists, who used the sanctity of life to abuse life. The Jews used the word of God to cover up their practice of selfishness and unconcern for the masses of humanity. They were forever seeking ways to justify their lack of concern for their fellow man by appealing to some text of God's law. For instance on one occasion, the Pharisees and Scribes came to Jesus and inquired of him, *"Why do thy disciples transgress the tradition of the elder? For they wash not their hands when they eat bread. But He answered and said unto them, 'why do ye also transgress the commandment of God by your tradition? For God commanded, saying, Honor thy father and mother: and He that curseth father and mother, let him die the death. But ye say, whosoever shall say to his father and his mother, it is a gift by whatsoever thou mightiest be profited by me. And honor not his father or his mother, he shall be free, thus have ye made the commandment of God of non effect by your tradition.'* (Matt. 15:2-6). Here is a classical passage, which they used to try to get out of expressing their kindness to their parents but instead blamed God for demanding of them the gift. They showed themselves to be very selfish and without compassion.

Down through the corridors of time, some of the greatest instances of cruelty and a total lack of mercy displayed has been the slaughter of thousands, both by Catholics and Protestants alike, in their quest to serve God. The inquisition and the response of the Protestant's reformation have seen the world's greatest atrocities all in the name of Christianity. It is no wonder that the words of Jesus, "I desire mercy" have such a strong pull on the lives of mankind. But before we embark on the study of the meaning of this word, what can we say of those whose quest for doctrinal purity and soundness more often than not overlook those qualities and virtues that exhibit the type of disposition that brings about a proper relationship between God and Man, as well as between mankind. How often is this Beatitude violated not only in letter but in spirit as well? How cruel have brothers been one to another in their quest to maintain what they considered doctrinal soundness, while they, without any pangs of conscience or feelings of remorse, systematically have gone after the total destruction of the character and soul of a brother or sister who may question some point of doctrine or who may disagree with some point of interpretation! How cruel and insensitive have we been one to another in the face of a criticizing world, who see us not as Jesus said that they would recognize us, (John 13:34-35) but rather because of our insensitivity and compassionate display of love one for another! Is there any blessed mercy left for us today? I believe that there is: Let us look at the word mercy and see if we can give an adequate definition and description of this word, then show the need that man has of mercy and see how this Beatitude extols and extends blessedness to those who are merciful.

The word merciful from the Latin word "miseriroidia" means pain of heart. In the Greek language it comes from the word Eleos which means kindness to the miserable, coupled with a desire to relieve. Pity especially on account of misery. Ubel Shelly says that mercy is the getting out of the narrow confines of selfish interest and moving into the larger world of caring for others and attempting to understand and meet their needs." Arthur Pink says: "mercy is an indispensable trait in the holy character which God has inseparably connected with the enjoyment of that happiness—both here and hereafter—which is the product of his own sovereign kindness". Thomas Scott says, "It is an aversion to everything harsh, cruel or oppressive or injurious; a propensity to pity, to alleviate or remove the misery of mankind; an unwillingness to increase personal involvement or indulgence by rendering others uneasy, a willingness to forgo personal ease, interest or gratification to make others easy and happy. "James Tolle says, "But in the fullest sense mercy is more than a feeling, it is also an action. It is not only the feeling of pain concerning the pains of others, with the desire to relieve their distress, but it is also the fulfillment of this desire in the active services rendered them. No one is truly merciful who stops at pity for afflicted, suffering men. Mercy is actualized outgoing good will and only those who express their pity and compassion in action are the merciful upon whom Christ pronounces his blessings. Therefore, we can deduct from these definitions that mercy embraces kindness, love and grace. It involves compassion and sympathy.

It is expressing our love and grace to those who are guilty of crime against God as well as us. It is sharing kindness to those who are in a miserable state of life. It is the simultaneous suffering with those who suffer. It is that sense of sympathy for those who are in sorrow or misery. Mercy is a feeling whose primary concern is with the heart. Mercy then involves an active participation. It is a word that describes an attitude of action about one who gets involved in the struggles, cares, and concerns of others. It is feelings in action. It is an active Good Will towards others. It is the results of the love of God being manifested in our lives towards others.

Jesus is the Personification of Mercy! The mission of Christ clearly and emphatically brings out man's greatest need. That need is God's mercy for His sins. Without this mercy he stands condemned and lost before the tribunal of God. He is guilty and without absolution. He therefore needs mercy. This mercy was supplied in the redemptive act of Christ as he shed his blood on Calvary for the sins of the world. Here was mercy's greatest extension, that in the cross of Christ, God accepted that sacrifice as the recompense for all of the sins of the world. And anyone who will come to Jesus on the terms he prescribed will receive this outpouring of mercy upon their souls. Listen to the Hebrew writer who not only shares with us the mercy of God on Calvary but shows that that mercy goes beyond the saving act and is applied to our everyday lives. *"Wherefore in all things it behooved him to be made like unto his brethren, that he might be a merciful and faithful High Priest in things pertaining to God, to make reconciliation for the sins of the people. For in that he himself hath suffered, being tempted, he is able to succor them that are tempted."* (Heb. 2:17-18) We must never lose sight of the fact that God is "rich in mercy" (Eph. 2:4). This mercy is for the vilest of sinners even he who considered himself "chief of sinners". (I Tim 1:15). He obtains mercy so all of us could know that no one is beyond the mercy of *God*, and that this mercy is made available to anyone on a continuous basis without fear of it ever running out. (I John 1:7)

How do we show our mercy to others? There are at least four distinctive areas in which we, as children of God, can show mercy to others!

ONE: In Being Benevolent

The Bible is emphatic about this element of being our brother's keeper. And there is no greater way to show our gratitude for the mercy of God in our lives than by being benevolent. In the life and ministry of Christ is exemplified in the eliminating of people's needs. And the apostles who wrote us our instructions are vivid and dogmatic in their appraisal of the place of benevolence in the life of a Christian. Listen to the apostle of love, John, *"But whose hath this world's goods and seethe his brother have need, and shuttled up his bowels of compassion from, how dwelleth the love of God in him?"* (I John 3:17).

James writes a commentary on this attitude when he said, *"If a brother or sister be naked, and destitute of daily food, and one of you say unto them, 'Depart in peace, be ye warmed and filled,' not withstanding ye gave them not those things what are needful to the holy, what doth it profit?"* (James 2:15-16) James had already made clear where benevolence stood in relationship to the mercy of God when he said: *"Pure religion and undefiled before the Father is this, to visit the fatherless and widows in their affliction..."* (Jas. 1:27a).

To visit here does not mean to make a social call but rather to relieve the burdens of those who have been robbed of support either by death or through *negligence*! Certainly who can refuse to see what role benevolent portrays when one hears the master tell of the criteria for judgment when He said in Matt. 25:31-46 that at the coming to be glorified there would be a separation of the sheep and the goats. Those on his right hand shall receive the eternal blessings of God and those on his left hand shall be consigned to eternal darkness. Notice the standard that Jesus said he would use: *"For I was hungry, and ye gave me meat; I was thirsty and ye gave me drink. I was a stranger and ye took me in. Naked and ye clothed me. I was sick and ye visited me. I was in prison and ye took me in."*

Those to whom the Master will say these things are going to answer in astonishment and ask, *"When did we do these things to you?"* Notice the Master's reply, *"...Verily I say into you inasmuch as ye have done it unto one of the least of these my brethren, ye have done it unto me."* Those who have been merciful to others shall receive the blessings of God.

Yet those who were not benevolent shall ask *"...Lord, when saw we thee hungered or thirsty, or a stranger, or naked, or sick, or in prison, and did not minister unto Thee?"* Notice the answer, *"... Verily I say unto you, inasmuch as you did it not unto one of the least of these, ye did it not to me."* Notice the criteria for judgment *"for he shall have judgment without judgment who hath showed no mercy and mercy rejoiceth against judgment"* (Jas. 2:13). Thus we must learn to show mercy to those in need. We must be like the Samaritan who went the second mile to show and share his mercy.

TWO: In Being Willing to Minister to the Spiritual Needs of our Fellow Men

What good does it serve to feed the stomachs and quench their thirst and put clothing on their backs and fail to feed them the spiritual sustenance to save their souls? We must remember why Jesus came to this world. We must not lose sight of the fact that He *"came to seek and to save that which was lost"* (Luke. 19:10).

To this end He endured the shame of Calvary and even in his efforts of benevolence He never lost sight of man's basic need, the spiritual relationship with God. We therefore must not lose sight of this need. We must always be ready to help our brethren from a spiritual point of view. How then do we show mercy in the spiritual realm?

First of all by being evangelistic. We must share the "good news" of the death, burial and resurrection of Jesus Christ with all mankind. Not to share the good news is to violate the trust of mercy. Notice what Jesus said to his disciples *"Whosoever sins ye remit they are remitted unto them; and whosoever sins ye retain, they are retained."* (John 20:23). If we do not tell them the good news then we retain their sins and if we retain their sins, then we are guilty of their blood. However, if we tell them and they respond in obedience then we have remitted their sins and we release their souls from the pits of Hell, and at the same time, we release our souls from their blood.

However, our responsibility does not stop here. Once they embrace the mercy of God, the Devil will pursue and seek to devour. When any of them be *"overtaken in a trespass"* (Col. 6:11) or if they "err" (James 5:19), then it becomes the responsibility of those who are spiritual to restore them in the spirit of meekness and fear." We must seek the restoration of these because they are weak in the spirit and they need to be helped.

How do we help those who are weak spiritually? We need to "equip" them (Eph. 4:12) and encourage them daily (Heb. 3:13) as we see the day approaching (Heb. 10:25). We must also rebuke sin in their lives (Matt. 18:15-17) so that they may allow Christ to be glorified in them "which is the hope of glory" (Col. 1:28).

THREE: In Showing Mercy By Making Intercessory Prayer

Intercessory prayer is one of the great privileges of being a born-again Christian. And the Master himself shows why. He prayed for His disciples (John 17). He prayed specifically for Peter (Lk.22), and as always, He prayed for the Sea of Lost Humanity. We must therefore learn to utilize the route of intercessory prayer for those who are not aware of their needs. It was Paul's desire that "...supplications, prayers, intercession and giving of thanks be made for all men" (I Tim. 2:1). Certainly the *"prayers of the righteous availeth much"* (Jas. 5:16b). We should remember to intercede on the church's behalf so that "we may lead a quiet and peaceable life in all godliness" (I Tim. 2:2). We should also pray for those who are being tempted, much like Peter who was being sifted like wheat by the Devil, but Jesus prayed much for him (Luke. 22:31). We should pray for the lost

(I Tim. 2:4; Rom.10: 1). We should pray even for our enemies (Matt. 5:43-45; Acts 7:60), and last but not least, we should pray for each saint, (Eph. 6:18).

FOUR: In Showing Mercy in Our Disposition to Forgive and Endure Wrong

In any form of relationship there will always be misunder-standings, and besides the Devil will always seek to stir up strife. It is here that the greatest act of mercy was shown both in the life of Christ and in the life of his early disciple, Stephen. It was on the cross that Jesus offered the words, *"Father, forgive them for they know not what they do".* (Luke. 23:24) If one could have seen what Jesus witnessed from his place on Calvary. If we could have some idea of the intense pain and humiliation that he endured, then we could have some idea as to the magnitude of his actions.

Similarly Stephen exhibited this type of attitude as he was being stoned to death, (Acts 7:60). Within this same example the apostle Paul calls upon us to exhibit this same disposition, *"Let all bitterness, and wrath and anger, and clamor and railing be put away from you, with all malice and be ye kind one to another, tenderhearted, forgiving each other, even as God also in Christ forgave you"* (Eph. 4:31-32). Here we see mercy in readiness willing to forgive. Certainly we must point out that the disposition and act are two different things. The offender through genuine repentance must seek forgiveness. But all Christians should have the disposition and willingness to forgive.

A Christian's forgiveness should show itself merciful with cheerfulness (Rom. 12:8). It should not be done grudgingly but rather with gleeful and joyous anticipation. It should express itself in the attitude of the father of the Prodigal. He rejoiced in that his son had returned home and he ordered the fatted calf and ordained a feast. As the Prodigal sought to show his humility and need of mercy, the father had already forgiven him! His love and concern for this young man had him to go against all acceptable standards of behavior for such a person of his status. Here we see a father who willingly violated the stated and acceptable laws of inheritance dividing his estate before he is ill or near death to both of his sons. The asking for the inheritance from a son to a father in this day and time was saying to the father, "I wish that you were dead!" Yet the father complied with the request in spite of the fact that both the sons violated all traditions of protocol—the youngest for requesting the inheritance and the oldest for not stopping the younger.

The young man leaves home and goes to the far country where he wasted his life with riotous living—living such a life that brought dishonor and shame to his father, race and culture. As he comes to his senses he recognizes that in his father's house there is enough food for him, the family and the servants. Returning home he is seeking to see which speech will he make that will best express his remorse, repentance and need of restoration. All of this will be unnecessary for his father is full of mercy. Here in application we see that those whose thinking is strengthened by the objectives of purity will see God. Because of this purity one will have the capacity, the ability and full assurance waiting to bestow mercy on his wayward children.

Yet of all of the statements Jesus has made thus far, no one is more challenging and more involved than this one. Why is this statement made here? Why not put it at the head of the list of these Beatitudes, instead of in the central part of the Beatitudes? When you stop and look at the purpose of all religion it would be to see God. It would be the ultimate goal of every redeemed child of God (I John 3:2). And yet Jesus, who does not just grab at random thoughts, places this one here at the middle. The first three Beatitudes lead up to it. The rest follow it.

When you consider the first three Beatitudes they deal with man's basic needs, his need of being spiritual—mourning for his sin, as well as those of others. He has a true understanding of having our power under the control of God. These three involve a deep awareness of our needs as we climb the ladder. As we climb the ladder we find that the next Beatitude God supplies our need "hunger and thirst after righteousness" "we shall be filled." That is we shall be satisfied. The following Beatitudes of being "merciful, pure and peacemakers" comes as a result of being filled with the righteousness of God.

Mourning Leads to Purity

In these Beatitudes there is a definite correlation between the cause and effect of each beatitude as expressed by Jesus. Mourning for one's sins especially as one relates to the righteousness of God would lead one to seek the very thing that has haunted mankind ever since the dawn of creation. Man is looking for that internal purity that allows him to feel valuable to himself and the rest of mankind and especially before God. But when man sees himself he can only see himself in his "natural state" or his "carnal state." Man is in need of purity of heart if he is to be with God.

MATTHEW 5:8

*Blessed are the pure in heart for
they shall see God.*

First of all this beatitude brings us to the realization that there are tremendous demands placed upon the disciples by Christ. Certainly in an impure world and age this beatitude becomes the most exacting of attitudes for all of us know the words of the prophet Jeremiah who said, *"the heart is desperately wicked..."* (Jer. 17:9). Why is the heart desperately wicked? David sheds some light on this subject when he wrote,*"Have mercy upon me, O God, according to thy loving kindness: according unto the multitude of thy tender mercies blot out my transgressions. Wash me thoroughly from mine iniquity, and cleanse me from sin. For I acknowledge my transgressions: and my sin is ever before me. Against thee, thee only, have I sinned, and done this evil in thy sight: that thou mightest be justified when thou speakest, and be clear when thou judgest. Behold,*

I was shapen in iniquity; and in sin did my mother conceive me.
Behold, thou desirest truth in the inward parts; and in hidden
part thou shalt make me to know wisdom. Purge me with hyssop,
and I shall be clean: wash me and I shall be wither than snow"
(Ps. 51:1-7). Mourning then becomes a tremendous basis by
which we reach out to God for his purging and purifying
substance. We therefore should realize how important being
pure is!

The Shocking Jesus

As one is confronted with the discomforting Jesus, He makes
the greatest demand that one can have made upon them as
members of the Human race! We must remember when Jesus
spoke these words; the world and those who heard must have
been taken backwards with such a pronunciation. The life of
the Jews had become nothing more than a ritualistic outward
formalistic activity. They were so manifestly concerned with
the outward observations that they actually disobeyed God
and his word, while thinking that they were the only ones who
truly understood God's law and kept it. It was within this
realm that Jesus gave his most scathing attacks and rebukes.
His confrontation with these people should teach us today to
beware that we do not become hard and listless in our services
to God! Notice what had transpired to the Jews in the days of
Jesus. Jesus accused the Jews of "saying" and not being "doers"

(Matt 23:3-4). "*Yea they bind heavy burdens and grievous to be borne, and lay them on men's shoulders; but they themselves will not move them with one of their fingers*". He charged them with showmanship (23:5) and prestige from men (23:6–7).

In verses 13–36, he makes accusations against them. He accuses them of . . .

1. Being "stumbling blocks" to those who are seeking the kingdom (verse 13)
2. Making men much more Hell bound than they were (verse 15).
3. Having words that lack sincerity and meaning (verses. 16-22).
4. Majoring in minors and minoring in majors (verses. 23-24).
5. lacking a proper sense of priorities and therefore being polluted (verses 25-26).
6. the sternest hypocrisy (verses. 27-28).
7. bigotry, prejudice, and for being responsible for the demise of the prophets (verses. 29-36).

What had brought on such a condition? They had exchanged the word of God and replaced it with the teaching and tradition of the Elders and the Scribes (Matt. 18:2). Their hearts had become insensible and hardened by the "deceitfulness of sin" (Rom 7:13). It is then to this mentality and way of living that this Beatitude is addressed. Certainly the purity of which Jesus spoke was one that was hardly spoken of in that day and time, and today our world especially —in what is known as the Western Civilization is far removed from the type of purity that Jesus is speaking of here.

D. Martyn Lloyd-Jones says: "We come now to what is undoubtedly one of the greatest utterances to be found anywhere in the whole realm of Holy Scriptures. Anyone who realizes even something of the meaning of the words, *"Blessed are the pure in heart, for they shall see God"* can approach them only with a sense of awe and complete inadequacy. This statement of cause, has engaged the attention of God's people ever since it was first uttered, and many great volumes have been written in an attempt to expound it...indeed no one can ever exhaust this verse. In spite of all that has been written and preached, it still eludes us. In order to even try to understand what Jesus said, we must try to evaluate what He did not mean. Jesus did not mean that those who did not suffer from physical diseases of the heart would see God. The heart that Jesus meant here must come from a deductive sense of reasoning. The heart of a man is a physical pump, a muscle. As a matter of fact it is the strongest muscle in the body. The heart is the most important organ to the body for it supplies the blood wherein life is located to every part of the body. The heart keeps a sustained and regular beat, which is essential to the prolonging and enjoyment of life. Without a proper functioning heart, all other parts of the body die. The heart pumps blood through veins and arteries. The blood carries the vital nutriments, which are necessary for the brain to function, as well as for the reproductive system of the body. No generation has been made more keenly aware of the heart's importance than ours. Heart disease is one of the nation's leading killers but Jesus is not speaking of an absence of heart diseases or of some blood related disease.

Jesus did mean that the "pure heart" was merely our intellect. The Pharisees knew every jot and title of the law but never grabbed its spirit. They did not recognize its spirit nor did they comprehend its principles, its justice, its mercies or its faith. It is possible to have an intellectual approach to the thing of God and to His word, without realizing that our response should also involve our "emotional heart." The Pharisees were all head and no heart. This is why Jesus could say: *"This people honored me with their lips but their hearts are far from me"* (Matt. 15:7).

Furthermore we do not believe that meant that the heart was just the "seat of our emotions". Certainly our feelings are useful in our day-to-day life. But feelings, without a proper understanding of the revealed wisdom of God, leads one to go about establishing his own set of righteousness and because of this many false doctrines. Yet it does not mean that we should eliminate that fact that emotions play a vital role in our faith and helps us to actualize and to move toward obedience to the will of God. A vivid example can be seen from the action of the Jews on Pentecost. Peter preached the gospel and when the Jews heard what he had proclaimed, they were *"pricked in their hearts"* (Acts 2:31). By the same token the emotions that lead one to obey will lead others to turn away from the truth like the Jews who contested with Stephen and in their blind emotions, stoned him to death.

What then is the heart that Jesus meant? I believe that the scriptures give us a picture of the type of heart that Jesus is speaking of. To Jesus the heart meant the center of the personality. The term heart does not merely mean the seat of the affections and the emotions. We must recognize that the Scriptures encompass all three when it speaks of the heart. The heart is the center of man's being and personality. It is the fount of which everything else comes forth. It includes the mind, the will and the emotions. It is that which comprises and makes a man *total*. It is what makes an individual think and act. In essence it is what makes a man! It was Solomon who said, *"Keep thy heart with all diligence for out of it are the issues of life"* (Prov. 4:23). Man must learn to guard his heart if he is to make it through life. The heart is the fountain of life and it is from the heart that happiness flows; therefore, it should be put in custody and kept. Jesus in his confrontation with the Jews of his day over the rejection of his miracles issued the most severe denunciation on unbelief when he said, "...for out of the abundance of the heart the mouth speaketh". (Matt. 12:34). It is those things, which proceed out of the heart of the man that brings about his defilement. Our actions and our activities are a reflection of what is on the inside of our hearts. The heart seems to be the target then of both God and Satan. If God can keep the doorkeeper of the heart, the eye, simple, then we have an enlightened heart but if the devil can cloud the eye, then darkness invades it and how dark then is the body! We must therefore guard it with all diligence as Solomon said. Why? Because Jeremiah said, *"The heart is deceitful above all things and desperately wicked: Who can know it?"* (Jer. 17:9). Why is the heart deceitful? Because it is the hiding place of sin. Listen to Jesus, *"For out of the heart preceded evil thoughts, murders, adulteries, fornication, thefts, false witnesses, blasphemies; these are the things which defileth a man: but to eat with unwashed hands defileth not a man."* (Matt. 15:18-20). It is then at the root of man's problems that Jesus wants to enter it. And it is why this Beatitude is so difficult to live—because it uncovers us and makes us search ourselves and question our sincerity!

What then does it mean to be "pure in heart?" In our day and time man is engrossed with purity. He is concerned that the air he breathes may not be pure enough or that the water he drinks may not be clean enough and even it our hygiene man goes to great lengths to maintain body cleanliness, yet somewhere along the line, man has lost sight of his need for purity of the heart. Over and over again the scriptures are resplendent with God's emphasis on purity. It was James who said, "...cleanse your hands ye sinners; and purify your hearts ye double minded" (Jas. 4:8). It was the globetrotting apostle Paul who instructed Timothy, "to flee youthful lust" (2 Tim. 2:19-22). To Titus when he had left at Crete, he said, *"To the pure all things are pure"* (Tit. 1:15). Peter admonished, *"But lives as he who called you is holy. Be ye yourself holy in all manner of being because it is written, ye shall be holy: for I am holy"* (I Pet. 1:15-16). God wants for us to be *pure*. We need to, however, discern what Jesus meant about being *pure*.

The word is "katharos" and it is found in the New Testament some twenty eight times. Barclay says that originally it simply meant, "clean" and could for instance be used of soiled clothes, which have been washed clean. He says that it was regularly used for corn, which had been winnowed or sifted and cleaned of all chaff. In the same way it is used of an army which has been purged of all discontented, cowardly, unwilling and inefficient soldiers and which is a force composed solely of first class fighting men. This word found in company with another Greek word, "akeratos"—can be used of milk or wine, which is unadulterated with water, or of metal, which has in it no tinge of alloy. Thus this word is "unmixed, unadulterated and unalloyed."

To the ancients it was used to express ceremonial purity as well as moral purity. In essence this Beatitude turns man's look inwardly and makes him come face to face with motive for self-examination of one's motives. And it is totally possible that we are not all free from fueling our lives with improper motives. Therefore we must truly understand this word and its subsequent teaching. Why then should we be pure?

1. To glorify our God, (I Pet. 1:14-16)
2. Because Jesus died to purify the church (Eph. 5:25-16)
3. Because our hearts will be judged (Acts 8:20-24),
4. Because if we are to achieve the ultimate— "seeing God"—we must be pure.

When you consider the somber words we must realize why God wants and will take only the pure in heart. It is because of the function, which the heart does. The heart thinks, reasons, and understands. It is from the heart that obedience springs from (Rom. 6:17-18). It is within the chambers of the heart that wills, thoughts, and purposes come forth, (2 Cor. 9:7). It is in the heart that true desires are born (Col. 3:1). It is within the heart that faith like a grain of corn seed dies and springs forth into new life (Rom. 10:9-10). It is from within the heart that our desires of right and wrong spring forth. Therefore it is necessary that it be a pure heart.

How then is the heart made pure? In order for our hearts to be pure we must have hearts that have been converted, consecrated and have allowed Jesus to be coronated. When we speak of the heart being converted, we are speaking of that regenerated process by which the heart is brought to life by the blood of Christ. Conversion takes place by the hearing of the gospel. This hearing produces faith (Rom. 10:17). Once faith is produced in man, he must repent of his sins (Luke. 13:3-5). That is he must turn away from the error of his ways and turn to God. This repentance comes as a result of the change of mind that takes place within the heart when one finds out that he has violated the laws of God and has sinned against the maker. This then compels one to change one's mind about sin and seek forgiveness. Once repentance has taken place one must then confess to the glory of the Father—that Jesus is Lord. Without this acknowledgment of Jesus as the Son of God, Christ will not accept us at His Coming (Matt.10: 32-33). This confession must be made publicly as a testimony of our faith. This confession is not of our sins but of our confidence and conviction that Jesus is the Christ, the son of the living God. Upon confession one is baptized for the "forgiveness of sins"

(Acts 2:47; I Cor. 12:13). Thus the process of purity of heart begins at the converted heart. However, in order to keep the heart converted, the heart must become consecrated. The terms "consecration," "sanctification," and "justification" all stem from the idea of holiness. It is this of which the Beatitudes speak. One must learn how to be pure in his "Mind" (Phil. 2:5), in His actions (John 4:34), in His desires (John 9:3), in one's obedience (Phil. 2:8), in one's attitude (Heb. 1:9) and in one's resolve (John 5:30). Only through the daily processes of dying to self and allowing the gift of God's son to dwell with one's spirit can consecration take place. You cannot wish to be consecrated. You must work towards it. (Col. 3:1) "Put it to death therefore." It is the setting aside of Jesus in our lives (I Pet. 3:15) that brings about this consecrated life.

Also, the heart must have a coronation of Jesus. He must rule, reign and guide. He, by God's decree, has been made "both Lord and Christ" (Acts 2:36). Except we submit to him he cannot be our King. Therefore, we must put him on the throne room of our lives and sit ourselves down on the footstool. How do we then do this? By *sanctifying in our hearts Christ as Lord!*" (I Pet. 3:15). It is a heart that surrenders to the Lord of Lord and King on Kings. He rules and abides within the heart!

The heart is made pure through conversion, consecration and coronation. But what then keeps it pure?

- We must guard our hearts (Prov. 4:2) for the Devil knows how sin is born. He knows that man is drawn into sin, *"When he is drawn away by his own lust and enticed,"* (Jas. 1:14). He therefore must keep his thoughts on things that *"are pure"* (Phil. 4:8). We must always be on guard that the devil does not infiltrate and cause our hearts to become evil because of unbelief (Heb. 3:12). Nor should we allow ourselves to be drawn into immorality, therefore, we need to put some distance between sin and ourselves. How do we do that?

- We must consistently check our motives. We must constantly make sure that what we do stems from a desire to be like Christ and not to satisfy our own egos and grandeur. We must not be so concerned for our own personal self that we exclude all others, thereby becoming selfish.

- We must not allow the spirit of jealousy or envy to divide us from our loyalties to God, but rather we must love others more than self (Phil. 2:2-3). Our disposition and our attitude should not be that of the elder brother of the prodigal in (Luke. 15:35). His jealousy and envy showed how little his father's joy or his brother's safe return meant to him.

- We must guard against pride, for *"pride goeth before destruction"* (Prov. 6:18). Pride will blind the heart to its true condition and will forever seal its doom.

- We maintain purity of heart by listening to what others hear us say:
  (a) We shall face God in the judgment and we shall be judged by our speech (Mt. 12:36).
  (b) Simply stated what's in the heart will betray itself through our speech, (Luke. 6:45).
  (c) Our speech is a gauge to our maturity or immaturity (Jas. 4:1-2).

Out of all of the blessings of the Beatitudes this is one that leads to much perplexity for it says something, which in other areas has been declared an impossibility. *"No man hath seen God at any time"* (John. 1:18). Moses was told by God, *"There shall no man see me and live"* (Ex. 33:20). Yet this Beatitude promises us that these blessings are to be enjoyed now. Certainly we acknowledge that there is a future fulfillment to this Beatitude (see I Cor. 13:8-9), but we must deal with the fact that this statement of Jesus deals with the here and the *now*!

We therefore understand that Jesus is not speaking of seeing God with the physical eye. With what eyes is Jesus therefore speaking? Paul sheds some light on this subject when he says *"having the eyes of your heart enlightened that ye may know what is the hope of his calling what the riches of the glory of his inheritance the saints"* (Eph. 1:18). The heart has eyes and it is with these eyes that the heart sees things that man with his natural eyes cannot see.

The eyes of the heart, when pure, are like the astronomer's eyes pitted against the untrained eyes. While the eyes of the astronomer can move the specific stars and constellations and see a variety of patterns and clusters of stars. The untrained eye only sees stars and is captivated by their illumination but does not know their name, constellation or grouping. So it is with those whose hearts are not pure. They cannot discern those spiritual values that help us to see God. They do not see the God of the universe in His handiwork, the Creation. They do not see God as the loving creator, sustainer and maker of the universe. They can neither comprehend the love and grace that drove God to create such a masterpiece, nor are they aware of the grand amount of blessings that He bestows upon humanity. We see God through the eyes of faith The writer of

Hebrews as he argues the fact that we see God by his creation also tells us that "by faith we understand that he world has been framed by the word of God." But the pure in heart are like the sweet singer of Israel who said *"I beheld the Lord always before my face for He is my right hand that I should not be moved: therefore my heart was glad and my tongue rejoiced."* (Acts 2:25-26). *"So that what is seen hath not been made out of things what appear."* (Heb. 11:3). We accept the fact that once nothing existed and through the divine set of God's creation power what is a result of what never had been.

The pure in heart see God working in the lives of man through His providential care. Look at Joseph's life and the lives of God's great servants as they went through the trials and tribulations of life and when they looked back at their lives, they like Joseph could say, "You meant it for evil but God meant it for good!"

The pure in heart see God working in the lives of man through His providential care. Look at Joseph's life and the lives of God's great servants as they went through the trials and tribulations of life and when they looked back at their lives, they like Joseph could say, *"You meant it for evil but God meant it for good!"*

The pure in heart understand that all of the trials and tribulations work for our own good and that these trials and tribulations which work for our own good cannot be compared with the glories that should be revealed hereafter (Rom. 8:18).

There is another explanation, which merits some consideration as one views the meaning of seeing God. In John 1:18 the words, *"No man hath seen God"* has before the word "God" in the Greek construction "the God" that is God in all of his power, substance. How in Matt. 5:8 *"...they shall see God"* has no definite article. This then could mean that if our hearts are pure then we can see God in Christ. This certainly harmonizes with passages that say, *"If you've seen me you've seen the Father"* (John 14:9). *"To wit God was in Christ reconciling the world..."* (II Cor. 5:19). Thomas' declaration, *"My Lord and My God"* (John 20:28) shows that he recognized God in Christ. This could be then the meaning that those who are unmixed in their hearts see God as manifested by the Lord Jesus Christ.

MATTHEW 5:9

Blessed are the peacemakers for they
shall be dalled the sons of God.

As Jesus pronounces his next step in the attitude of those who are members of his kingdom, a possible state of shock must have overcome his Jewish hearers. They had been waiting for the Messiah to come and to overthrow those who had his people in captivity. Here then was the expectant Messiah, speaking of peace and pronouncing a blessing upon those who were *makers of Peace*!

As the progression of the Beatitudes is revealed we are keenly made aware of their interdependency. Just as mourning brings purity as we are made aware of meekness leading to peacemaking. As we recall from our earlier discussion, meekness is not weakness as some have counted it, but we have seen that quite the opposite is true. Meekness is strength in control. As we look at meekness it has both a passive and active aspect.

In its active sense meekness is anger at sin, whether it is in our lives or in the lives of others with an unselfish motive. In its passive sense it is the joyful acceptance of God's will for our lives. Meekness is therefore characterized both by war and peace. We are at war against sin and we have peace with God. It is the proclamation of God's commands for holiness, and acceptance of the price of maintaining holiness in the midst of sin.

As we speak of being peacemakers we must concur that peace is also a result of knowing that the blood of Christ has cleansed us. Therefore "purity of heart" is also a prerequisite for being a peacemaker. Thus we find that the first three beatitudes have to do with our needs. That need is satisfied in the fourth, the next three are a result of that being filled. First there is "poverty of spirit" that leads to "mourning" which leads to "meekness". These needs are satisfied in "hungering and thirsting" which helps to realize how merciful God has been to us. We therefore show "mercy". Because of the reception of mercy in our lives we find that "purity of heart" that helps us to see God. Once this takes place who, can but speak for the *Master!*

As we look at this Beatitude we must first of all look at the need for peace. Man is in need of peace. This need of peace stems from the results of man's biggest problem. "The heart is desperately wicked." The problem of the heart is the heart of the problem. What is the problem? It is sin. *"For all have sinned and fallen short of the glory of God"* (Rom. 3:23). The problem of missing God's highest mark is that it separates God from man. This separation comes as a result of God being the *"God of the living, not of the dead."* The sinner is dead in the sight of God. Ezekiel said, *"The soul that sinneth, it shall die"* (18:4, 20). Paul said, *"The wages of sin is death...."* (Rom. 6:23) "because sin separates which is the same as death" (Isa. 59:1-2). It makes man a fugitive from God, and evokes a declaration of war from God (Gen. 3:15) between himself and the Devil's seed. Since sin is a barrier between God and man, it must be viewed as a serious matter. Sin at its worst is not only the "breaking of God's law" (I Jon. 3:4) but at its most heinous when viewed as the "breaking of God's heart" (Gen. 6:1-5). Because of the serious action of trespassing, man therefore stands guilty before God. Since he cannot face God in this guilty situation he must flee from God's presence. It was this guilt that caused Adam to flee from the presence of God in the Garden of Eden. He knew that he had broken God's expressed commandment and stood ashamed before Him. Sin therefore makes all of us guilty. It was Paul's conclusion (Rom. 3:10, 23). The entire human race stands before God guilty of sin. Sin then is the great robber. It robs man of the sweet fellowship that he has with God. It breaks up personal relationships and brings about guilt before God.

It is because of this guilt that man desperately searches for peace. He is at war with God, and he cannot do anything in and of himself to remove that guilt. Since God is the offended party then the terms of peace and the condition for peace are solely God's. To this end the Gospel of Christ is the Magna Charta of that peace. Jesus is the peace of God. Yet man whose greatest need is peace with God must forever be on the lookout for the proper type of peace. Peace must never be seen as mere personal contentment or compromise. Our purity of heart and meekness will not allow us to seek peace at any price. The child of God will not compromise the principles of righteousness and holiness just to have tranquility. This is not peace. As a matter of fact, peace "at any price" is nothing more than a covering for future problems.

What type of peace is the peace that man needs? We can honestly say that the type of peace that man needs lies in three areas:

1. He needs peace with God.
2. He needs peace with himself.
3. He needs peace with his fellow man.

Of these three, certainly the most important is peace with God. Then self. Then fellow man.

In order for man to have peace with God, man needs a mediator. He cannot come to God on his own for he does not have the credentials to stand before a holy God, as he is!

God in His infinite wisdom and mercy knows this. Therefore, God made the proper provision for man's problem. That problem –sin— was remedied at Calvary. *"For it was the good pleasure of the Father that in Him should all the fullness dwell: and through Him to reconcile all things unto Himself having made peace through the blood of his cross: and you, being in times past alienated and enemies in your mind in your evil works, yet now hath He reconciled in the body of his flesh through death to present you holy and without blemish and unreproveable before Him."* (Col. 1:19-22). Again peace is made available in Christ, *"Being therefore justified by faith we have peace with God through our Lord Jesus Christ."* (Rom 5:1). How is peace achieved through the cross? The cross of Christ satisfies the demands of a perfect and just God. That demand was for a sinless sacrifice made through unblemished blood. Jesus Christ met this demand. He was sinless (John 8:24); His blood was pure (I Pet. 1:16-19). He therefore is God's satisfaction and appeasement (I John 2:1-2). On the other hand he is what man needs—The Perfect Substitute. His life and sacrifice fulfill the demands of man. Therefore as we hide in "His blood". His blood stands before God pure and unblemished. Then that which is hidden is the blood has the perfect assurance of eternal salvation. Therefore man has peace.

The second type of peace that man needs is with him. Man, as he stands before God, stands condemned without the blood of Christ. With the blood of Christ he can be justified because his sins are forgiven. However, in order for man to truly have peace with himself, he must learn two things:

1. To forgive himself
2. To live by faith

The guilt of man before a righteous God can cause man to become proud of being so evil that he cannot find it in himself to forgive himself. In this state he will not allow himself to be free and have the peace that passeth all understanding. Man needs to realize that God understands how horrible guilt will make us feel. Yet it is precisely here that man must learn to trust God and to recognize that God has the ability, as well as the capacity, not only to forgive but also forget. Therefore he should learn to bask in the glow of a peaceful atmosphere. God has forgiven. God has forgotten.

This brings us to our second point. Peace is through faith. It comes as a result of our relationship with God. We can therefore say that peace is a by-product of our relationship with God, which is based on faith. Paul understood this and so he triumphantly says, *"I have been crucified with Christ and it is no longer I that liveth but Christ liveth in me: and the life which I now live in the flesh, I live in faith, the faith which is in the Son of God, who loved me and gave himself up for me!"* (Gal.

2:20). The life of faith, which results in inner peace, is a life of total commitment to the cause of Christ and calls for total surrender of myself. Therefore, this life manifested itself because it *"walks by faith"* (2 Cor. 5:2), and we know that its salvation is *"by faith"* (Eph. 2:8-10). We also know that we live by faith (Gal. 2:20), we are justified by faith (Rom. 5:1), and therefore our peace is based on our faith. The greater our faith, the greater our peace. Since we live by faith, we therefore understand that our lives before God are based on faith and we accept all of His provisions by faith!

Third, man needs peace with his fellow man. Certainly our world can attest to the fact that if ever peace was needed between men, it is now. Yet one can have peace with God and peace with self without having peace with man. Certainly peace is desirable for all of mankind. That's why we have had the "League of Nations" and the "United Nations" and the different counsels for world peace. Yet in our world there is very little peace with man. The reason being peace with someone else is impossible when I don't have peace with myself. The resolutions of these worldwide organizations will never bring fruit of a lasting peace, for peace begins with the acknowledgment of the supremacy of God. But not all believe the report of God as found in the Scriptures. However, the Scriptures teach the child of God to try to be at peace with all of mankind. *"If it be possible, as much as in you both, be at peace with all men,"*

(Rom. 12:18). God expects that peace with everyone will not be possible but he nevertheless expects his followers to *"...follow after the things which make for peace..."* (Rom. 14:18). The question how do we follow after the things that produce peace? Paul tells us in Rom. 12:9-21 *"Let love be without hypocrisy. Abhor that which is evil. cleave to that which is good. In love of the brethren be tenderly affectionate one to another; in honour preferring one another, in diligence not slothful; fervent in spirit; serving the Lord; rejoicing in hope; patient in tribulation, continuing steadfastly in prayer; communicating to the necessities of the saints; given to hospitality. Bless them that persecute you, bless and curse not. rejoice with them that rejoice; weep with them that weep. Be of the same mind one toward another. Set not your minds on things high, but condescend to things that are lowly. Be not wise in your own conceits. Render to no man evil for evil. Take thought for things honorable in the sight of all men...avenge not yourself, beloved, but give place unto the wrath of God; for it is written, vengeance belongeth unto me: I will recompense saith the Lord. But if thine enemy hunger, feed him. If he thirst, give him drink, for in doing thou shalt heap coals of fire upon his head. Be not overcome of evil, but overcome evil with good."*

When a man's ways are peaceful even his enemies will speak well of him. Certainly this is God's formula for attaining peace with mankind. God does not expect for man to be at peace with all of mankind if these conditions are not present.

Thus peace with God is attained because of Christ and through Christ. Peace with self is a by-product of that relationship we have with God and peace with our fellow man is conditional.

What then are Peacemakers? The Greek word for Peace is "Eirene". The Hebrew counterpart is the word "Shalom". Neither of these words conveys the thought that peace is the absence of conflict and strife alone but it describes also serenity, prosperity and happiness. It carries the idea of right relationships, friendships, and fellowships. When the ancients said "Shalom" to a person leaving, they were not just wishing him an absence of conflict but they were wishing for him all that God blesses man with. It was a term that was inclusive of every blessing of God and for every known favor. Therefore when Jesus pronounces a blessing on the peacemakers he is doing so because peacemakers are trying to bring those who are at war with God, fugitives from God, into a proper and right relationship with God. When hostilities cease, fellowship and all of the blessings that go along by being in a right relationship with God are fully *restored!*

Who then can be peacemakers? There are some qualities that peacemakers must possess in order for them to be truly peacemakers. These qualities are found only in those who have come to be pure in heart. This purity of heart comes through the process of being lowly, or humble, meek or having one's strength under control and by having the fruit of patience. These things are accomplished when we have a new outlook, a new view of ourselves and a new view of the condition that this world is in. These things will then motivate us to seek the peace of God for all of mankind. This will constrain us to go into the highways and byways to seek those who are at war with God.

What are the results of being peacemakers? We shall be called Sons of God. Since God is a God of peace (Rom 15:13,16:20), then all those who are seeking to be peacemakers will be recognized and shall be known as God's sons or as God's children, which carries an affectionate tone and denotes the consummate relationship between man and God. As God's children then we are his heirs and joint heirs of the Prince of Peace. We possess all the blessings that God has to *give*. Every possible blessing that God will give his children will be recognized—because God, guided by the Spirit of God, possesses the peacemakers and they are not content to allow the Devil to win their souls.

Peacemakers are truly blessed. They are ones whose life and disposition are friendly, zealous of good works and are always striving to bring about peace and harmony between God and man.

MATTHEW 5:10

*Blessed are ye, when men shall
revile you, and persecute you, and
shall say all manner of evil
against you falsely, for my sake.*

If there was ever a paradoxical statement in the beatitudes then this is it. Why would Jesus state right after he elaborates on the blessedness of being a peacemaker that there be persecution to endure by those who are peacemakers? That there is somewhat of an issue here none can deny but within the context of this beatitude and the following verses we shall see a definite correlation and outcome that is just as natural a progression as breathing air and drinking water. The entire beatitude comes full circle with the promise made to those who would endure the persecution that Jesus speaks of. This persecution must be understood in the light of what Jesus said and not in the light of what is often thought of as persecution. We must look at this text with the eye of scrutiny and not seek to find things that Jesus neither said nor implied. This is a strange yet magnificent beatitude and it deals with the fact that these beatitudes are spiritually oriented and spiritually centered in the life of the disciple. When we therefore look at this beatitude we will see clearly what Jesus did not say as well as what Jesus did say. We will see why someone can be blessed even when one is undergoing the different types of persecution that Jesus said would come to the disciple. And then we will see how one can find the enormous blessings in the withstanding of persecution for the sake of Jesus Christ.

What we need is to understand, in light of this beatitude is:

- Why are we persecuted?
- Who persecutes us?
- How does persecution become a blessing?

Christians are persecuted because they are a certain type of people and they behave in a certain manner. We have been called to be different than the world we live in and to proclaim that difference not only in action but also in word. The disciple of Christ must understand that he is a "stranger in the world, an un-welcomed guest and a disturber of the peace. No wonder the world rejects them. *"Beloved since all the beatitudes describe what every Christian disciple is intended to be, we conclude that the conditions of being despised and rejected, slandered and perse-*

cuted, is as much a normal mark of Christian discipleship as being pure in heart or merciful." Every Christian is to be a peacemaker, and every Christian is to expect opposition. Those who hunger for righteousness will suffer for the righteousness they crave. We should not be surprised if anti-Christian hostility increases, but rather be surprised if does not.

Matthew Henry in His commentary says: "this is the greatest paradox of all, and peculiar to Christianity, and therefore last and more largely insisted upon than any of the rest...they are persecuted, hunted, pursued, run down as noxious beast are they sought to be destroyed as if a Christian bears a wolf's head. They are to be fined, imprisoned, banished, stripped of their estate, excluded from all places of profits and trust, scourged, racked, torture, always delivered to death and counted as sheep for the slaughterer. This has been the effect of the enmity of the serpent's seed against the Holy Seed ever since the time of righteous Abel."

Of the things that the New Testament confirms is the fact that "... all that would live godly in Christ shall suffer persecution" (2 Tim. 3:12). Over and over again Jesus foretold his disciples that they would be persecuted: in the teaching of the destruction of Jerusalem Jesus had told them "Take heed to yourselves: for they shall deliver you up to councils; and in the synagogues ye shall be beaten: and ye shall be brought before rulers and kings for my sake, for a testimony against them".

(Mark 13:9). Again in the same teachings about the destruction of Jerusalem as recorded by Luke, Luke gives us more graphic details about the impending persecution. "But before all these, they shall lay their hands on you, and persecute you, delivering you up to the synagogues, and into prisons, being brought before kings and rulers for my name's sake" (Luke. 21:12). In Luke 21:16 Jesus further enumerates this persecution by saying, "and ye shall be betrayed both by parents, and brethren, and kinsfolks, and friends: and some of you shall they cause to be put to death". James Tolle, in his book on the beatitudes, shows us that history has confirmed this. He says God's decree that His children shall be persecuted has been confirmed throughout the history of Christianity, and the Lord's predictions concerning such persecution have come to pass as he said. Since the earliest days of the church, valiant Christian men and women have been thrown in prison and put to the sword, the fire, the lion and the torture. Not long after the establishment of the church, persecution broke out when Peter and John were hailed before the Sanhedrin and threatened with punishment (Acts 4:1-22). Later all the apostles were brought before the council and given a flogging (Acts 5:17-24). Shortly after, the first Christian martyr Stephen was stoned to death by an angry mob of Jews (Acts 7:54-60). Then *"there arose on that day a great persecution against the church which was in Jerusalem"* (Acts 8:1). The primitive church continued to face persecution. Paul speaks of the persecution he personally suffered: *"...in prisons more abundantly, in stripes above measure, in deaths oft. Of the Jews five times received I forty stripes save one. Thrice was I beaten with rods, once was I stoned..."* (2 Corinthians 11:23-25).

After these persecution there would come the type of persecution that was instituted on an empire basis and would seek to ultimately destroy the church of Christ. Its greatest test came under the reign of Domition from 81-96 AD. His persecution was one of savagery and inhuman treatment. Under the reign of Diocletian and others, persecution was also prevalent. Thus faithful Christians must remember that they *will* suffer persecution! Also the church is persecuted when the church is the church. It is bound to be the conscience of the nation and the conscience of society. Where there is good the church must praise, where there is evil the church must condemn and invariably men will try to silence the troublesome voice of conscience.

One thing that we need to understand is what this text does not say. This text does not say blessed are they that are persecuted because they are objectionable people who are the type of people that bring about persecution because of their attitudes and their disposition, as well as their actions. These are they who go out of their way to be antagonistic and complain when their very actions bring about persecution.

The Bible is clear that persecution should be because of rather than instead of. Peter in his epistle of I Peter says *"But rejoice, inasmuch as ye are partakers of Christ's sufferings; that, when his glory shall be revealed, ye may be glad also with exceeding joy. If ye be reproached for the name of Christ, happy are ye; for the spirit of glory and of God resteth upon you: on their part he is evil spoken of, but on your part he is glorified. But let none of you suffer as a murderer, or as a thief, or as an evildoer, or as a busybody in other men's matters. Yet if any man suffer as a Christian, let him not be ashamed; but let him glorify God on this behalf"* (4:13-16).

The second thing this text does not say is blessed are they who are having a hard time in their Christian life because they are being difficult. These are they who cannot get along with others because they so opinionated that they give no one else an opportunity to voice theirs. Or they make the faith so difficult to comprehend and to live that they cause frustration and people respond in a negative manner by persecuting them. The text does not say so.

Third, the text does not say blessed are those who are being persecuted because they are seriously lacking in wisdom and are really foolish and unwise in what they regard as being their testimony.

What this text does teach us is that the persecution comes because of righteousness sakes. In other words what Jesus says here is that the cause of persecution is on account of, because of the cause of righteousness. This reason eliminates all other reasons for being persecuted. The term righteousness must be understood in light of our concept and the Biblical concept as found recorded upon the pages of inspiration.

The term righteousness from the term (dikaiosune) implies a moral, ethical and spiritual concept. These concepts are based on the fact that there are some things that are wrong and there are some things that are right. What is right must be based on some standard. In the Bible the standard of righteousness is God. These standards are based upon the character, the nature, the personality and the integrity of God. If God is righteous it is because he has all sovereignty of right and wrong and therefore cannot be mistaken. In light of the total righteousness of God man must recognize that he has fallen short of that perfection of God, therefore he is in need of help, especially grace and mercy.

Thus God has provided a way in which man can live righteously even though he himself lacks the qualities that would make it possible for him to be totally righteous.

There is also a double aspect of righteousness. There is both a permanent and a changing element. The fixed element is that there are some things that will be right, thus the concept to do right. Then there is the changing concept of what may be right at different times and at different circumstances.

Certainly the Christian concept has always maintained itself on the fact that there are certain things that will never change no matter how the society changes!

Let us remember that no amount of external practices that do not emit from the internal spirit of man will be acceptable to God. If we really want to understand the righteousness of God, then we need to look at two of many pictures that will give us a true picture of what righteousness is not and what it is.

The best picture of what righteousness is not can be found in the classic enemies of Jesus the Pharisees. These Pharisees had an outward manifestation of doing what was right based on their understanding of the law. These Pharisees were the by-product of Zealots whose concern was for the letter of the law and not the spirit of the law. Thus their concept of righteousness was mere formality with attention being made to outward details of the law without any regard for the spiritual indwelling principle of the law. Thus, they could justify their outward conduct while thinking evil and irrational internally.

Of the many confrontations that they had with Jesus none was more bombastic, chiding and demeaning as the one that is recorded for us in the 23rd chapter of the Gospel of Matthew. Here the Lord issues eight (8) woes to the Pharisees and followers. He accuses them of being Lazy and pretentious, boastful, haughty and duopolistic; loving the salutation of men and their recognition. Then beginning in Verse 13 he accuses them of blocking the kingdom of God to those would enter it. In Verse 14 he accuses them of profiteering by "devouring the houses of widows" and pretentious by their long prayers. In Verse 15 he berates them for their false missionary zeal that destroyed people rather than converting them. In Verses16-22 he accuses them of a gross lack of integrity because of their lack of proper priority, proper vision, proper direction, proper understanding, proper honor for the God that made the things that they denounced. In Verses 23-24 He chides them for lack of understanding the weightier things of the law. In Verses 25-26 He accuses them of gross internal corruption. In Verse 27 he accuses them of the vilest hypocrisy. In Verse 28 He accuses them of pretentious and ostentatious commitment to outward things particularly the death of the prophets, the tombs of the prophets while in reality they were guilty and accountable for the death of the prophets. For this Jesus says to them that they were nothing more than serpents, vipers and that the condemnation of hell awaited them. Thus, we see that the external righteousness for which the Pharisees were famous; Jesus condemns and pronounces the greatest anathema on them. They were not what they professed to be.

The second factor that helps us to understand righteousness is the fact that some five hundred years after God had made the first covenant with the Jews, He called Jeremiah and through him prophesied a coming new covenant where the law would be written internally in the heart of men and not like the old written on tablets of clay (Jer. 31:31-34), thus indicating that the Spirit of God's Word would be on the inside of a person and thus motivate that person from within rather than from any external influences or factors. This New Covenant would be enacted upon "better promises" and righteousness would be imputed rather than being meritorious. This righteousness would be by "faith" rather than by law keeping and works of merit.

Ever since the implementation of the New Covenant the righteousness of God has been based on the internal ness of God's Spirit and not on the external, thus deepening the obligation to do right.

So when Jesus says for righteousness sake, he is speaking of the motive for doing what one does. This motive comes from a singleness of purpose, aim and conviction. The internal workings of the Holy Spirit through the usage of the word motivate us to act in accordance with the things of God and does not require external prodding or help from without. Thus the persecution that Jesus is speaking of is that character or quality of being right or just; it carries with it the idea of being free from duel motives and concludes by having an attitude that looks for the things that please God. It is motivated by what God considers to be the right thing to do. It is always seeking to fulfill the expectations of God and not the expectations of men. It is the capacity to live right, walk right, speak right and do right at the right time. It is godly behavior and proper comportment.

Thus the believer is for-warned that they shall suffer persecution because:

- They are not of this world, they are called out of the world; they are separated from the world.

- Believers strip away the world's cloak of sin. They live and demonstrate a life of righteousness. They do not compromise with the world and its sinful behavior. They live pure and godly lives. They have nothing do with the sinful pleasures of a corrupted society.

- The world does not know God or Christ.

- The world is deceived in its concepts and beliefs of God. The world's concept of God is one in which he is seen as an old decrepit grandfather who protects, provides and gives no matter what a person believes or how he behaves.

What type of persecution will one receive? There are three types of persecution mentioned by Jesus in vs. 11:

- Being reviled—that is being verbally abused, insulted, scolded and mocked.
- Being persecuted—that is being hurt, ostracized, attacked, tortured, martyred and treated with hostility.
- Having all manner of evil spoken against you—that is being slandered, cursed, and lied about.

What should be the believer's attitude towards persecution? It is *not* to retaliate; it is neither to be arrogant, full of boasting nor to act spiritually superior to others. Rather one should rejoice and be glad, (2 Cor. 12:10; 1 Peter 4:12-13). Why? Because the persecuted are promised great rewards. The kingdom of heaven is given unto them.

- They experience special honor (Acts 5:41).
- They experience special consolation (2 Cor. 1:5).
- They experience a very special closeness, a glow of the Lord's presence.
- They become a great witness for Christ (2 Cor. 1:4-6).

CONCLUSION

The Blessed life is thus a transformation from the natural to the supernatural, from the physical to the spiritual, from the selfish to the generous, from the self-righteous to the imputed righteousness of God, from the braggart to the meek, from the proud to the humble, from the self reliant to the God dependent, from the ordinary to the extraordinary, from a life dependent on circumstances to a life dependent on God.

The blessed life is then a life of understanding where true happiness resides neither in the possession of things nor in the accumulation of those things nor in the possession of worldly wealth. It understands its needs to submit to a higher power. It is a life that understands its weakness to rid itself of its sinful nature and therefore lives a life of mourning over its own inability and the rest of the worlds. It is a life that understands its need to surrender its strength and live under the control of a greater power. It is a life that is not satisfied with what it accomplishes today in the pursuit of righteousness but starts every day with until its life is filled with the complete righteousness of God.

The blessed life is a life in pursuit of the purity of life and has no mixed motives in its approach to life. Everything it does stems from a pure motive in life to honor, glorify, and exalt the Lord Jesus Christ. It is a life that is lived in the singleness of life's pursuit.

The blessed life constitutes in the disciples understanding the responsibility and the purpose of Christ's coming to the earth. That purpose was to remove the enmity that existed between God and man, (Gen. 3:15) and to provide man with a ministry of reconciliation (Luke. 19:10). In this understanding he recognizes that he must join ranks with the son and become a peacemaker between man and God in order to remove and eliminate the chiasm between the two. In so doing the disciple understands that the natural outgrowth of his attempts and striving to help others become free from the tyrannical power of Satan's revenge will be to be persecuted. His blessedness comes from one being counted worthy to suffer for the sake of Christ.

Finally the blessed life is the life of an attitude and disposition based upon the quality of life that one possesses as a result of one's relationship with God. This relationship will allow one to see himself as he truly is. He will see himself as utterly sinful before God and the need to humble one's self in order to walk with God. The blessed life is about victory through surrender. It is not about the forfeiture of life but the acquisition of true life. It is man's ability to extricate himself from his unnatural environment to live a productive, satisfying and meaningful life. The blessed life is the attainment of that utopian life that so many covet and never achieve usually ending up in a nightmare of life. The blessed life is about joy, peace and overcoming that produces a healthy, spiritual relationship not only with God, but also with the rest of humanity. The blessed life is the complete life for it brings us full circle to the God that we abandon and from whom we became fugitives. It is like the prodigal son who has found his way back home to his father's house.

BIBLIOGRAPHY

1. Barclay, William *"Matthew"* Daily Study Bible Series, The Westminster Press, Philadelphia, Pa. 1976

2. Guelich, Robert A, *"The Sermon on the Mount, A Foundation for Understanding",* Word Book, Waco, Tx. 1982

3. Jones, Martyn Lloyd D *"Studies in the Sermon on the Mount"* Wm B. Eerdmans Publishing Company, Grand Rapid, Michigan 1985

4. Kell, Ted *"Study Notes, Sermon on the Mount"* Sunset International School of Biblical Studies, Lubbock, Tex. 1970

5. Pink, Arthur W. *"An Exposition of the Sermon on the Mount,* Baker Book House, Grand Rapids, Michigan 1985

6. Sewell, John C. Ph D *"The Gospel of Matthew"* Landmark Publication, Ashland City, Tenn.

7. Stott, John R.W. *"The Message of the Sermon on the Mount"* Inter-Varsity Press, Downers Grove, Ill. 1973

8. Tasker, R.V.G. *"Matthew, The Tyndale New Testament Commentaries"* Eerdmans Publication, Grand Rapid, Michigan 1983

9. Toll, James A. *"The Beatitudes"* Haun Publication Co. Pasadena, California 1966

10. Vines, W. E *"Am Expository Dictionary of New Testament Words"* Fleming H. Revel, Old Tappan, New Jersey, 1966

11. Wiersbe, Warren W. *"Be Loyal"* Victor Book House, Wheaton, Ill 1982

12. Zodihates, Spiro *"The Pursuit of Happiness"* AMG Publication, Chattanooga, Tenn. 1970

CPSIA information can be obtained
at www.ICGtesting.com
Printed in the USA
BVHW031335260423
663002BV00007B/574